A Gift For:

. . . .

From:

. . . .

Retire
HAPPY!

...

An Inspiring Guide
to the Rest of Your Life

GIFT BOOKS
from Hallmark

CONTENTS

INTRODUCTION

Chances are, you have worked an average of 90,000 hours toward your retirement but have spent only about ten hours planning for it. Currently, about eighty million baby boomers are approaching this important transition. And it can be an exciting, exhilarating, wonderful, fearful, emotional place to be!

Because there's more to retirement than money, this book goes beyond the traditional issues you've been facing and delivers a balanced and comprehensive look at what retirement really means. This is not the kind of stuff you're likely to get from your financial advisor—but it's the kind of stuff that's likely to affect your life profoundly, such as how to spend your time in the most productive, satisfying ways and feeling healthy, happy, and young at heart. From travel to volunteering to weekends with the grandkids—there's sure to be something that inspires you.

Retirement may (or may not!) be the ending of working, but it's just the beginning of living. And we hope this book will inspire you to live your retirement to the fullest—in a way that's exclusively, happily, perfectly you.

PART ONE

...

What shall you do
with your retirement?

RETIRE HAPPY

. . .

"Don't simply retire from something;
have something to retire to."
–Harry Emerson Fosdick

To paraphrase the Temptations, "Get ready, 'cause here we come!" With longer life spans, better health, more education, and greater geographical mobility and affluence, those of us approaching retirement or recently retired are reshaping the meaning of retirement itself.

Retirement is a fairly recent phenomenon; at the beginning of the 19th century, few people retired, because they simply could not afford to do so. As white-collar jobs replaced a predominantly agricultural economy, however, incomes rose, and people had more money with which to retire. They lived longer and had more leisure activities from which to choose. The advent of Social Security and pensions also contributed to the ability to retire.

Today, however, the conventional definition of retirement itself needs to be retired! Before the baby boomers, retirement was seen primarily as a male's onetime passage from the workforce, and research concerning retirement dealt almost exclusively with men. Retirement was viewed more in isolation, as a solitary passage, though the reality is that most retirees are married. Retirement is now recognized as a process, involving perhaps several forays into and out of alternative projects, pastimes, and jobs. And now that almost half the workforce is female, retirement is no longer a male phenomenon; it's also recognized as more of a couples' issue.

We frequently hear predictions by pundits and the press about how the future of retirement will resemble the past of retirement. That is, in the future as in the past, we will work until we die. The news contains innumerable anecdotes about middle-aged workers losing their nest eggs (or having a "cracked" nest egg or not having one at all). Surely each of us could add tales from our own acquaintances, if not ourselves, to the list. The stories make interesting news, but the facts point in a different direction: We are spending more of our lives in retirement than at any time in history, which is a trend that's projected to continue into the foreseeable future.

REAL RETIREES

Let's take a look at three couples to see how the concept of retirement has changed.

Mike and Mary (born 1900; retired 1965): Lucky to be alive! The very idea of retirement must have seemed peculiar to Mike and Mary. Certainly none of their forebears were likely to have lived long enough to provide an example of retirement. With a life expectancy of about 47 years, neither Mike nor Mary should have anticipated living long enough to retire, but they defied the odds and lived well past their working years. In fact, Mike and Mary would live through our collective awakening to the idea of "life after work."

Retiring in 1965, Mike and Mary would have felt lucky to be alive. Moreover, their admittedly modest (possibly nonexistent) expectations about retirement surely would have been exceeded. During their working years, it would have been unfathomable to them that, at age 65, they would be able to stop working yet continue to receive a check and have something enjoyable

> FDR signed the Social Security Act into law on August 14, 1935. In January 1940, Ida May Fuller became the first recipient of Social Security benefits. And did she ever benefit! Ida lived 35 more years, and she collected more than $22,000 before finally giving out at the age of 100.

to do in their leisure years.

Ken and Doris (born 1920; retired 1982): A well-deserved respite. Ken and Doris came of age during the Great Depression, when a quarter of all workers were unemployed. Their defining life experience was undoubtedly World War II, when Ken was shipped overseas to fight the Nazis as an officer in the venerable Eighth Air Force, while Doris stayed at home to work as a typist at the local aircraft assembly plant. After the war, Ken began his civilian career as a mechanical engineer at the Company, and Doris left the formal workforce to pursue the business of raising her children and keeping house. Ken toiled loyally for the Company over the next 38 years, earning his steady pay raises and sharing in the economic success of both the Company and the country during the expansionary years of the 1950s and 1960s.

Ken and Doris no doubt possessed a strong work ethic born of their experiences both in weathering the Great Depression and in fighting the war. But Ken and Doris were also human, and they wanted to retire at a reasonable age in order to pursue the life of leisure. Gladly for them, retirement was swiftly becoming an institution in the United States, and when the couple retired in 1982, they could have reasonably expected to live in leisure for 18 or so years. Moreover, they would be able to afford a comfortable retirement. During the 1950s, Social Security benefits increased by nearly 80 percent, truly helping to make retirement an entitlement. Additionally, in the sixties, the Company introduced a pension plan to provide postretirement income to its employees. Medicare became a reality in the sixties as well, providing healthcare benefits to older people. Ken and Doris had cause to feel financially secure about retirement, as did many of their contemporaries. In fact, during the 1960s, about 50 percent of all Americans were covered by private pension plans in addition to Social Security. That must have been nice, but then again, their respite was hard earned and well deserved.

Bob and Cindy (born 1950; retiring circa 2010): The retirement "boom." The baby boomers are only now beginning to retire, and yet we are reminded of this demographic phenomenon at every turn. No single topic, save perhaps the dying sport of shuffleboard, is more commonly identified with retirement than is the demographic fact of the baby boom. Most commonly, we hear the dire predictions of a bankrupt Social Security system or of intergenerational strife caused by the increased financial burden on future workers required to subsidize the retirement of the boomers.

Though these concerns are real, Bob and Cindy are likely to enjoy a long and prosperous retirement, relative to that of prior generations. Because of the steady increase in life expectancy, Bob and Cindy could enjoy 30-plus retirement years, longer than any group of retirees in history.

Though the terms "leisure" and "retirement" call to mind images of relaxation, Bob and Cindy are not likely to spend the second half of their lives idle. The most important questions about their retirement relate to how and where they will spend their time. Whereas previous generations were lucky to see retirement at all, the current generation of retirees can safely expect to spend a significant portion of their lives retired, but probably not merely relaxing—perhaps working, and certainly not bored.

Because both the duration and nature of retirement have changed, Bob and Cindy need the resources to plan adequately for an active, emotionally satisfying, and financially secure retirement.

Imagine you have reached this milestone called retirement. Envision your typical day. Is it spent walking on the beach, playing tennis, or golfing? Are you volunteering? Pursuing an advanced degree? Working, like 80 percent of boomers aged 45 and older expect to do (based on a survey by AARP)? Doing absolutely nothing?

The good news is that 92 percent of US retirees report being very happy or quite happy, according to a 2005 survey conducted by AXA Financial. So is there a perfect time to retire? Are there secrets to a successful retirement? Recent scientific studies involving the psychology of retirement address our current realities of this important time and can provide practical suggestions for achieving a successful and satisfying retirement.

TIMING IS EVERYTHING

To work or not to work? Ignoring financial considerations for the moment (we'll address them in Chapter 9), the psychological research is a bit inconclusive about work after retirement and its effect on well-being. In a nutshell, it just depends!

There are two competing outlooks. The first, continuity theory, is the perspective that our levels of self-esteem and life satisfaction stay the same, independent of work. Under this theory, it wouldn't matter whether a person worked; he or she would maintain the same feelings of well-being. The second perspective, role theory, has two sides. Although role theory considers working to be paramount to a person's identity, retirement can improve feelings of well-being if the career being left was considered very difficult or stressful; or, retirement can cause distress if people feel they have lost a valuable role by not being employed. It turns out that the effect of leaving the primary career is more a function of how you perceived that career—that is, whether working played a crucial role in your life, was something to give up with relief, or was immaterial to how you thought about yourself. Consider the following studies.

REASONS TO RETIRE

In a survey of more than 700 soon-to-retire, newly retired, and retired men and women, participants in the Cornell Retirement and Well-Being Study were asked their reasons for retiring. Their responses:

Women

- To do other things (69%)
- Financial incentives (40%)
- Have enough income (38%)
- Spouse retired (33%)
- Older worker policy (24%)
- Poor health (24%)
- Didn't like work (24%)
- Didn't get along with boss (22%)
- Family health (21%)
- Not appreciated (19%)
- Job ended (7%)

Men

- To do other things (70%)
- Financial incentives (62%)
- Have enough income (45%)
- Didn't like work (33%)
- Older worker policy (22%)
- Poor health (21%)
- Didn't get along with boss (19%)
- Not appreciated (17%)
- Family health (16%)
- Job ended (13%)
- Spouse retired (9%)

This ranking gives some insight into the when of retirement. The desire to do something else and the perception among both the men and the women that they were financially able to retire were paramount. Note that for women, however, the fact that their spouses retired was a much more motivating force to retire than it was for men. While virtually all those surveyed had done some planning for their retirement, more than half felt they had not planned enough. So here's a word to the wise: Plan ahead.

Working can provide rewards and satisfaction such as status, intellectual engagement, social interaction, purpose, feelings of pride and accomplishment, structure, and, of course, a paycheck and health coverage. Regardless of your reason for retiring, whether you stop working entirely, cut back on hours, or pursue other endeavors such as volunteering, enjoying a hobby, or cultivating a skill, you will still want to experience these rewards in your everyday life.

> According to the Life Events Scale, which ranks 42 life events from most stressful (death of a spouse) to least stressful (minor law violations, such as a parking ticket), retirement ranks 10th!

In another study, 17 employed and 54 retired professors, aged 70 to 74, were interviewed to determine the reasons some retired and some continued working. Whether deciding to retire or remain employed, both groups reported high levels of satisfaction with life, although the employed faculty ratings were higher (97 versus 90 on a scale of 100).

For those who remained employed, the primary reason was because they enjoyed their work (77 percent). Other factors included work being important to them (35 percent), financial issues (12 percent), and inertia (6 percent). For those who retired, the primary reasons were a desire to do other things (35 percent) and because it was time (35 percent). Additional factors included changes in the work environment (24 percent), tired of work (20 percent), health issues (17 percent), and could afford to retire (13 percent).

Interestingly, there were more married couples among the retired group than the working group, and the retired group also had more children and grandchildren than those who were employed.

This study is noteworthy because it removes the entire issue of having to leave the workplace (there was no mandatory retirement age). There's no one right answer to the question "When should I retire?" The answer can partially be determined by the role work plays in a person's life, as well as the satisfaction that working provides. The reasons to work or not work were primarily psychological, and unlike in the Cornell survey mentioned earlier, financial aspects played a minor role in deciding whether to retire.

ARE YOU READY TO RETIRE?

For each question, choose the statement that best fits your thinking and frame of mind at the present time. More than one answer may seem appropriate, but you must pick only one.

1. **How do you feel about giving up your job and career?**
   a. My career is history. I'm ready to open a new chapter.
   b. I would enjoy meeting other retirees from my profession.
   c. I would like to stay up to date with trends and developments in my profession just to keep my hand in it.
   d. Once retired, I'll be happy to mentor younger people in my profession.

2. **How open are you to new adventures in your retirement?**
   a. I'll probably do things I've done in the past, but now I'll have more time for them.
   b. I'm itching to try some things I never had time for during my career.
   c. I don't plan on changing my leisure activities that much.
   d. I earned my retirement, so I'm going to have fun doing nothing.

3. **What part will exercise play in your retirement?**
   a. My outdoor activities will keep me in good shape.
   b. I'll keep my weight in check by walking.
   c. I plan to have a regular daily exercise program.
   d. I probably won't have a planned exercise program.

4. **Do you plan to include weight training?**
   a. Weight training may do me more harm than good.
   b. Weight and resistance training will be part of my exercise program.
   c. I'll get enough exercise through aerobic activities.
   d. Bodybuilding for seniors doesn't make sense to me.

5. **How home-based will your retirement be?**
   a. I'll spend a lot of time at home doing at least one of these activities—watching TV, talking on the phone, doing household chores, working on the computer, and reading.
   b. Chilling out at home is my idea of retirement.
   c. If I am home too much, I have to get out.
   d. I expect to spend a good deal of time carrying on activities outside the home.

6. **How does your spouse's retirement coincide with your own?**
   a. My spouse has already retired.
   b. My spouse does not plan to retire any time soon.
   c. My spouse and I plan to retire together (within an 18-month period).
   d. I don't have a spouse.

7. **What is the status of your children?**
   a. I still have children living at home.
   b. I have no children living at home.
   c. I have "boomerang kids" who may want to return home for a while.
   d. I have no children.

8. **Are you at risk for depression?**
   a. I have suffered bouts of depression in the past.
   b. My spouse has had some problems with depression.
   c. I have no history of depression.
   d. I get anxious now and then and down at times but not what you'd call clinical depression.

9. **Are you a "hobby person"?**
   a. I have no major hobbies, but I may find one during retirement.
   b. I have some hobbies to keep me busy.
   c) I don't really need any hobbies to enjoy retirement.
   d. There is at least one current hobby that I can devote more time to during retirement.

10. **How active are you in community organizations?**

   a. I'm not a joiner.

   b. I plan to become active in some organizations once I retire.

   c. I'm already active in several church/social/civic organizations.

   d. I belong to some organizations, but I'm not very active.

11. **Do you like volunteer work?**

   a. I already do volunteer work when I find time.

   b. I have other activities that keep me busy and don't need volunteer work.

   c. I prefer to work for pay.

   d. I plan to volunteer some of my time during retirement.

12. **What friends do you spend the most time with?**

   a. I have close friends from work and outside of work.

   b. I make friends easily, and my time with them varies widely.

   c. I spend as much as half of my social time with friends I know from work.

   d. I spend only a small part of my time socializing with work friends.

13. Do you have a good support network?

   a. I have at least five close friends that I see often.
   b. My social circle includes more than a dozen good friends.
   c. I enjoy my own company and am not really a social person.
   d. I have one or two friends I see regularly.

14. How will travel play a role in retirement?

   a. I enjoy travel more than my spouse does.
   b. I enjoy being close to home.
   c. I enjoy travel and look forward to many trips during retirement.
   d. My spouse enjoys travel more than I do.

15. How important is family time in retirement?

   a. I look forward to family visits during retirement.
   b. I plan to spend more time with family during retirement.
   c. Visits to family members won't play much of a role in retirement.
   d. Visits to my spouse's family are too frequent or too long.

16. Do you and your spouse (or significant other) enjoy doing things together?

   a) We don't have the same interests.
   b) We have some interests in common.
   c) We like doing things together and separately.
   d) I don't have a spouse or significant other.

17. Will learning and studying play a role in retirement?

   a. They may play a role if I find something I like.

   b. I finished school a long time ago. Why go back to the classroom?

   c. My spouse or friends have encouraged me to take some courses.

   d. Taking courses on various subjects will make retirement more interesting.

18. How's your work/play ethic?

   a. I earned my rest, so I don't plan to work at anything too hard.

   b. I'll throw myself into my retirement just as I did my work.

   c. The less work, the less the stress in my retirement.

   d. I won't mind work as long as it's not too taxing.

19. Will you be acting your age during retirement?

   a. Now that I'm older, I will be restricting some of my activities.

   b. I expect health problems will have some effect on my retirement.

   c. For the immediate future, I expect only a few physical limitations.

   d. I don't feel my age. Mentally, I am decidedly younger.

20. Does the TV keep you company?

    a. On a typical day, I have regular TV shows
       I watch.

    b. I watch TV but I prefer to be doing other things.

    c. On a typical day, TV is my main source
       of entertainment.

    d. I watch TV fewer than 3 hours a day.

21. How easily will success come in retirement?

    a. I succeeded in my career and I'll be just as
       successful in retirement.

    b. I will have to change gears and think differently
       in retirement than I did during my career.

    c. Succeeding at retirement may take a little work.

    d. I'm not really sure.

22. Will you have enough money for retirement?

    a. Good financial planning will pave the way
       for my retirement success.

    b. I plan to work part-time to make sure ends meet.

    c. I'm not sure how financially prepared I am.

    d. It will be touch-and-go on the money,
       but I'll get by.

23. Will your native skills help you in retirement?

    a. I'm still at the top of my game.

    b. I'm not as mentally sharp as I was 20 years ago.

    c. Retirement means I won't have to push
       myself, so I'm not concerned about skills.

    d. Employers don't want an over-the-hill
       person like me for good-paying jobs.

24. How's your health?

a. Good. No chronic diseases, and the same for my spouse (if you have one).

b. I'm okay, but my spouse has a serious health problem.

c. I have some health issues, but my goal is to not let them slow me down.

d. My health is a problem and may seriously affect my retirement activities.

25. Are you prepared for retirement?

a. I've been looking forward to it for a long time, so I'll be okay.

b. Of course. I don't have to prepare for goofing off.

c. I've planned a few things that should be fun.

d. I've done a lot of planning and research on what I will do with my time.

Scoring

1. (a)4 (b)2 (c)1 (d)2
2. (a)3 (b)4 (c)1 (d)0
3. (a)3 (b)3 (c)4 (d)0
4. (a)0 (b)4 (c)3 (d)0
5. (a)1 (b)0 (c)3 (d)4
6. (a)4 (b)0 (c)4 (d)2
7. (a)0 (b)4 (c)2 (d)4
8. (a)0 (b)0 (c)4 (d)3
9. (a)2 (b)3 (c)1 (d)2
10. (a)0 (b)3 (c)4 (d)1
11. (a)4 (b)2 (c)2 (d)4
12. (a)3 (b)4 (c)1 (d)2
13. (a)3 (b)4 (c)0 (d)1
14. (a)1 (b)0 (c)4 (d)1
15. (a)4 (b)4 (c)0 (d)1
16. (a)2 (b)0 (c)2 (d)4
17. (a)2 (b)0 (c)2 (d)4
18. (a)0 (b)4 (c)0 (d)1

19. (a)2 (b)1 (c)3 (d)4
20. (a)1 (b)3 (c)0 (d)4
21. (a)2 (b)4 (c)2 (d)2
22. (a)4 (b)3 (c)3 (d)2
23. (a)4 (b)3 (c)0 (d)0
24. (a)4 (b)0 (c)0 (d)1
25. (a)2 (b)0 (c)3 (d)4

Total Points:

Below 50—Abort your retirement mission immediately. Key systems are not functioning properly.

50 to 59—A launch hold is in effect. More preparation is recommended.

60 to 69—A launch is possible but prepare for a bumpy ride.

70 to 85—You're cleared for takeoff. A few system checks and repairs may be necessary during the flight.

Above 85—A-OK. All systems are a go.

Reprinted with permission of www.retirementrocket.com.

GENDER AND RETIREMENT

Research has shown some common threads about the effects of retirement and working (or not working) on couples. One study looked at transitions in retirement involving 534 married couples in their fifties, sixties, or seventies who were retired, or about to retire, from several large businesses in upstate New York.

Husbands and wives reported greater marital satisfaction if they retired at the same time. While men with nonworking spouses had greater marital satisfaction than those with working wives, regardless of whether the men themselves worked, those men who didn't work but had working spouses reported the most marital conflict. Women experienced the highest marital satisfaction if they entered new jobs after retiring and their husbands were also working, but men who worked after retiring from their primary job experienced more marital discord than those men who didn't work.

You may have heard the saying "Twice the husband but half the money." According to Ronald J. Manheimer, executive director of the North Carolina Center for Creative Retirement at the University of North Carolina, women's fears in retirement include losing one's identity (becoming more prevalent with the increase in the number of retiring professional women), being responsible for their spouses'/significant others' social lives and entertainment, experiencing a disruption of their established patterns, needing to take care of everyone, financial and health issues, and outliving their spouses. Men's concerns include lack of status, lack of social support, lack of purpose, declining physical abilities, poor communication with significant others, and boomerang kids.

On the flip side, women's fantasies include returning to school, becoming an entrepreneur, beginning meaningful volunteer activities, renewing relationships, and enjoying life. Men's dreams include an active lifestyle, getting in shape, reviving romance with their spouses, increasing involvement with their grandchildren, and developing new skills. Both men and women include travel on their wish lists.

The first two years of retirement are comparable to the first two years of marriage or parenthood; it's a time to negotiate (or renegotiate) roles and share ideas and dreams. As when getting married or having a child, it's important to discuss and plan for the future before retiring, from an emotional as well as a financial standpoint. Realize that the transition to retirement is a period of marital challenge for both sexes. Take heart—although there are lots of adjustments to be made, 60 percent of couples report that there is (ultimately) an improvement in their marriages after retirement.

If the role of work is important to you but is causing stress in the relationship, take a look at alternative forms of work. Work doesn't necessarily mean only paid and full-time work. It could include volunteering, community service, working fewer hours, doing projects, or starting a new, scaled-down career. All of these could fit the definition of productive work. In the United States, success tends to be defined in monetary terms, but separating success and productivity from paid employment will create many more options for making retirement a time of new and meaningful roles.

EASING THE TRANSITION

Obviously, retirement brings about a shift in roles and activity. People who can adjust and adapt to these changes will have a more successful transition to retirement. But what personality traits facilitate the easiest transition? Research indicates there are two chief ways of looking at the world that increase the chances for smooth sailing through this choppy time: an internal locus of control (the belief that outcomes are under one's control) and retirement self-efficacy (the belief or self-confidence that one can cope with the changes retirement brings). Here are some tips to help ease the transition, no matter which outlook on life you adopt.

Consider moving to neutral ground. Shortly before retiring, Brian and Joanne K. sold their home and moved to an active-adult community in their same town. This had the unintended but positive effect of creating a new environment that was free of their previous territorial patterns (her kitchen, his garage).

Take action. Demonstrate that you believe outcomes are under your control (even if you don't) and that you are confident you can cope with retirement changes (even if you aren't). For example, if you're married, be willing to go beyond conventional gender-based roles. Renegotiate! Consider housework or yard work. Take, for example, Shelley and Marty L. Marty is a recently retired CPA, and Shelley recently sold her college prep-test business. While they were both working, they employed a cleaning service for their home. Now that they are retired and have decided they could do this themselves, Marty cleans the house every Wednesday while Shelley golfs in a women's nine-hole group. After two years, so far so good. Or look at Joanne and Craig C. Craig has a demanding career in IT, and Joanne has the demanding role of running their household, which consists of four (three of whom are now grown) children, two dogs, and a cat. However, the one thing Joanne detests is cooking. In their retirement planning, they have decided on what they call the "twice a day" rule—and no, we're not talking about sex. Joanne and Craig have agreed that when Craig is retired two years from now, Joanne will make two out of three meals a day, but that's it. A third meal will be eaten out, ordered in, or cooked by Craig. Joanne wants to retire, too!

Develop resilience. Resilience, the ability to bounce back after adversity, is an important ingredient in the recipe for successful retirement. It is possible to cultivate this quality. Accept that change is part of life; concentrate on changing adverse circumstances that can be altered; act decisively rather than wishing problems would just disappear; maintain perspective; take big problems and break them into smaller, manageable challenges; foster positive relationships; and take good care of yourself.

Consult others. Discuss how your friends and relatives in the same situation adjusted (and compromised and renegotiated) during this transition period. Consulting with a counselor or couples' therapist, a life coach or a trusted religious leader, and/or attending seminars on retirement (if they include more than just financial issues) may help if there is difficulty transitioning.

Saddle up! Right after retirement, retirees report an increased energy level. Use this "honeymoon period" to your advantage and plan, plan, plan.

ON BEING SINGLE

You may have been single all your life or ended up single as a result of divorce or death. According to Elizabeth Holtzman, MSW, MA, at the University of Massachusetts in Amherst, there are some psychological aspects that relate specifically to being a single retiree.

"Being single both simplifies and complicates the problems of retirement," she says. "It simplifies them because you have only yourself to look after; you can make your own choices. On the other hand, you don't have a partner to share things with or lean on emotionally or financially. Being a single retiree may lead to isolation and loneliness."

Luckily, there are tangible ways to combat these psychological considerations. For one, you can choose to live in a location that is single-friendly. Some specific places include Sarasota and Naples, Florida; Las Vegas; and Asheville, North Carolina, and there are many others. And consider taking your friends with you! We have met a number of singles in the same socioeconomic group who look at possible places for relocation together. They'll already have a social nucleus in their new home.

Another way to combat loneliness is to join a social-support group, which is equally as important for couples as it is for singles. If you've stopped working or you relocate to a new area, isolation could become an issue. Consider moving into an active-adult community that has built-in social activities or a master-planned community with a club-house or center that offers planned get-togethers and outings. Other options include returning to paid employment, volunteering, checking out the local senior center, starting or working on a hobby that involves people—in other words, joining in! One easy, free way to share your interests with others is Meet-up (www.meetup.com). This is a free Internet site that allows you to get together with others (perhaps at a library, Starbucks, or park) who share similar passions. Simply put in your zip code and see what groups are out there, or start your own Meetup group. See Part 2 for more specific suggestions.

As a single, since there is no financial backup, it's especially important to begin your retirement planning early. If you're a woman, this is particularly true, since women generally are paid less than men, may have been out of the workforce for years to raise children, and may or may not have the funds to support the retirement lifestyle they would like. It's a good idea to seek professional advice now from a certified financial planner or a CPA to begin the planning process.

BELIEVE THAT YOU HAVE
ENOUGH MONEY

The perception that you have enough money to retire has a bearing on your feelings of satisfaction concerning retirement. In one study, more than 1,000 people age 55 and over were surveyed about their satisfaction in retirement. The study found that satisfaction increased with the number of years a person saved for retirement. Of those who saved for 25 years or more, 60 percent said they were "extremely satisfied" with retirement, as did half of those who saved for 15 to 24 years. Less than half of those who saved for fewer than 15 years could report the same feeling.

Note that the correlation is between feeling financially prepared and feeling satisfied in retirement, regardless of actual net worth or wealth. So save, save, save!

Research at Penn State University determined that it's not the absolute amount of money a person has that contributes to feelings of happiness; rather, it's the comparison of income level with one's peer group. The researchers call this a hedonic treadmill, since incomes tend to rise over time, and people have to spend more energy to "keep up with the Joneses." The study also found that physical health was the largest predictor of happiness, followed by income, level of education, and marital status.

Studies also show that people who place a high priority on the pursuit of money and the accumulation of material things are more depressed and suffer from lower self-esteem than those who make relationships their top priority. Trite but true: Money really can't buy happiness!

HAVE A SUPPORT SYSTEM

How important is it to be connected to others? According to the research, very! Two studies illustrate how vital social support really is.

The 22-percent effect: Lynn Giles, PhD, and three other researchers followed 1,500 older people for ten years and found that those with extensive social networks outlived those lacking social support by 22 percent. Interestingly, it was friends and not relatives who had this effect. (This is not to say relatives aren't important; they just weren't a factor in increasing longevity in this study.) The effect of friends increasing life span persisted, even when those in the study experienced huge changes such as the death of family members or a spouse.

The two-and-a-half-year effect: One 13-year study, involving 2,812 men and women in New Haven, Connecticut, 65 years of age and older, investigated the relationship between social activity and longevity. It found that men and women who were socially active lived an average of two-and-a-half years longer than those who were not socially active.

This study is important because it links a longer life span to activities such as playing cards, eating out, or going to movies with others, without regard to physical exercise. It had been widely thought that activity prolonged life because of the physical aspect; now we know that social engagement alone can increase the life span. That doesn't mean you can retire to the couch, though!

Why do friends increase longevity? Although

the research doesn't answer this question, perhaps friends encourage their friends to take care of themselves, seek medical help when necessary, model coping mechanisms, or lift their moods.

Women might have an easier time reaping the benefits of social support because they tend to cast their nets wider than men when choosing friends. Men tend to find their friends at work. So what's a guy to do? Give these ideas a whirl: group activities such as watching or participating in sporting events, attending spiritual retreats, joining organizations such as model railroad clubs, eating out with others, and volunteering.

DON'T WORRY, BE HAPPY!

Recently, psychologists have taken to identifying people who consider themselves happy and examining what traits they share. This focus on a wellness model, rather than a disease model, has resulted in some interesting findings.

One recent study investigated the relationship between positive thinking and the risk of frailty. The researchers followed 1,558 older adults for seven years and compared frailty (determined by speed of walking, strength of grip, weight loss, and fatigue) and measured positive thinking by asking participants how many particular positive thoughts they had over the course of the study (such as "I felt hopeful about the future"). As a group, frailty increased among the aging adults, but those with positive emotions and thinking were less likely to become frail.

Previous research has shown that positive

thinking can decrease the time required to recover from serious illness, and it lowers the risk of strokes and heart attacks. A study that followed 545 men for 15 years found that the most optimistic men in the group were half as likely to die from cardiovascular disease than those men who were least optimistic. Talk about the power of positive thinking! Why does it work? A few possibilities have been proposed. Positive emotions may directly influence body chemicals in a way that affects health. Positive people tend to have increased social interactions, which may result in more access to resources. And positive people may be better at coping with and addressing problems.

University of Pennsylvania psychologist Martin Seligman, PhD, has been studying happiness and optimism for more than 25 years and suggests we go beyond seeking pleasure and instead look for gratification. What's the difference?

Pleasure is not necessarily meaningful and does not always result in a greater good. (For example, eating a piece of cheesecake may feed your stomach, but not your soul.) Gratification involves cultivating and nurturing your strengths and putting them to positive use. Consider Darla and Jim W., whose first child died just prior to childbirth. Although devastated by the loss, they set up a foundation at a local hospital to provide indigent women with the financial resources to bury children who died under similar circumstances. Darla and Jim took their strengths of compassion, generosity, and financial savvy and parlayed them into a gratifying experience in the midst of their sorrow. Likewise, we can cultivate happiness by incorporating strengths such as kindness, humor, optimism, and courage into everyday life.

To become a happier person, Dr. Seligman suggests you find your calling. A job provides a paycheck; a career provides power, prestige, a paycheck, and a personal commitment; but a calling is a passion where the activity itself is its own reward regardless of any status or income it may provide. A calling can be any line of "work," be it caregiver, artist, spouse, or engineer. It's a matter of finding an activity that provides challenges that mesh with your unique strengths.

Another way to become happy is by learning to see the glass as half full. "Pessimists tend to have hopeless thoughts, or worse, they stamp themselves with a negative label, such as 'jerk,'" says Dr. Seligman. If this sounds like you, he suggests speaking to yourself as a close friend would. Tell yourself that you learned from the experience and will do better the next time. And rather than name-calling, try something like, "Sometimes I'm not as considerate as I'd like to be, but overall, I'm a kind person." Dr. Seligman coined the term "learned helplessness"— giving up because you feel you can't change outcomes—and says we can escape this belief with "learned optimism."

He advises "not to ruminate about bad events that happen to you. . . . I recommend fun distractions, because studies show that if you think about problems in a negative frame of mind, you come up with fewer solutions." Plus, you're more likely to become depressed. Pessimists can overcome this cycle, though, and train themselves to think more optimistically—once they boost their moods. "It takes most people a few weeks to get the knack, but once the technique is learned, the less likely they are to relapse," says Dr. Seligman.

So put a stop to distorted ways of thinking. When you think something negative, note it, evaluate it, and replace the thought with something more realistic. It takes practice, but it's an effective tool for increasing happiness.

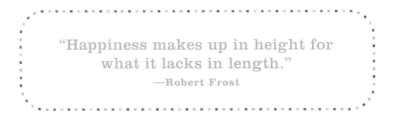

"Happiness makes up in height for what it lacks in length."

—Robert Frost

ACCENTUATE THE POSITIVE

Here are some specific suggestions for boosting your mood.

- Accept yourself as you are, and accept that you deserve to be happy.
- Live joyfully in the moment. Do today what you would do if you found out you had only months left to live. As comedienne Grace Hansen noted, "Don't be afraid that your life will end; be afraid that it will never begin."
- Help others, and ask for help when you need it. Be able to answer the question: "What did I do for someone else and for myself today?"
- Plan pleasurable activities in advance. Looking forward to something is a mood-brightener.
- Just do it! Though most of us believe that we must change our attitudes before we change our behaviors, the reverse is also true. Behaving in a desirable way can actually change your brain's chemistry and thus affect your way of thinking.
- Be aware of stereotypes. Negative attitudes about aging are believed to begin in childhood; many people grow up with erroneous beliefs about getting older. If you have a jaundiced view of aging, knowing the origin of your feelings may help to change them.
- View the world optimistically.
- Foster an internal locus of control for your successes and an external locus of control for your failures. Locus of control, a concept developed by Julian Rotter in 1966, refers to

how you perceive the outcomes of certain events. People with an internal locus of control generally believe that personal actions are responsible for outcomes, while those with an external locus of control attribute outcomes to forces beyond their control (fate, luck, society, etc.). We have to be realistic, however, and recognize when failure is due to lack of effort or our own limitations. And of course, sometimes things may truly be beyond our control!

• Laugh often, smile frequently, and look for the humor in daily life. Work at being curious, realistic, and flexible. Remember, you cannot always control what happens to you, but you can control your response.
• Cultivate a sense of wonder about the world.
• Think of five things each day for which you are grateful—and write them down.

HEALTHINESS EQUALS HAPPINESS

Sure, you feel better when you're well, but it's the physical act of exercise that brings about a shift in mood. A psychological bonanza of more pleasurable feelings results from just a short investment of time. In one study, men and women, average age 53, completed surveys before, during, and after a 15-minute walk. Everyone reported a more positive effect (feelings or emotions) and greater energy, both during and after the walk, and felt greater calmness and relaxation 15 minutes after completing the walk.

Healthwise, marriage really is for better or for worse! If one spouse has high blood pressure, high cholesterol, depression, asthma, ulcers, or arthritis, the other spouse is much more likely to suffer from the same disease. Couples tend to share many lifestyle choices, such as nutrition, exercise, smoking, drinking, and work habits. They also tend to share such factors as emotional stressors (financial problems or dealing with children), allergens, and other environmental risk factors. People tend to marry people like themselves—similar backgrounds, education levels, and economic status. It turns out that this holds true for health status as well. One study of more than 4,700 married men and women between the ages of 51 and 61 investigated the relationship between spouses and health status. The researchers found that men aged 51 to 55 who are in excellent health have barely a 5 percent chance of being married to women in fair health and just a 2 percent chance of being married to women in poor health. Bottom line: We choose spouses whom we can not only grow old with but whom we can grow old well with.

Health is not just an individual matter. As Sven Wilson, the study's author, points out, "Household matters!" Taking stock of your present health situation as a couple may provide a window to your future health. Since each of you shares the same environmental conditions, psychological stresses, and behavioral patterns, the concept of spouses tending to mirror one another's health level is something to consider as you plan your retirement. For example, knowing that your spouse is in poor health in his or her fifties could be the impetus to purchase long-term care insurance or perhaps help determine where you live—staying near family or choosing a location near excellent medical facilities.

John K. retired early. Here is his story.

I started working for my company at the age of 20. It was my first and last full-time job for more than 35 years. I realize it is not typical anymore, but none-theless, it afforded me the opportunity to experience retirement at a relatively young age.

The day I retired, I was happily living in Atlanta, Georgia, and didn't particularly want to change the lifestyle I had grown accustomed to. While working, I was responsible for the retirement of thousands of individuals at a major corporation. We would inform employees who were retiring or simply planning for a future retirement of benefits they had earned while employed. During the course of retirement planning, I would hear individuals' concerns as they approached their ultimate decision at the end of their working careers: Should I retire now, can I afford to retire now, what would happen if I stayed just a little longer? At my company, and I suspect at most major corporations, you might be putting yourself in a pre-carious situation if you even hint at retiring. What does it mean to your position? Am I putting my job and livelihood in jeopardy? This particular decision is totally individual and no amount of discussion with others can totally alleviate the fear of the unknown. I can think of only a few situations and a few lucky people who can be rather calloused toward retirement. They are generally the ones with exceptional skills or knowledge who would have no difficulty in reentering the working world; but for the rest of us, when the door closes, entry back through the same door at the same compensation level is virtually unheard of.

I'm now 57, and along with my wife, Janet, I am now retired and living in a little slice of paradise in Florida. Surprisingly, for someone as heavily involved in the retirement process for as many years, I spent relatively little time planning for my own pending retirement. Like the proverbial auto mechanic who drives a vehicle in need of repair, my wife and I seemed to put others first, and at the end of the day, found our own plan lacking.

Nonetheless, here we are, having relocated to what we believe is our dream location in a small city within an hour's commute from a major city, just far enough away not to be a bedroom community to the busy working world. We live near the ocean, near our golf club, and near the fitness center that we use, surprisingly, several times a week.

I was blessed to work for a company that offered its employees the opportunity to take an early retirement, and I was fortunate enough that it afforded me the opportunity to leave at age 55. But, I wondered, should I retire?

Up until the summer I was to retire, I was still having trouble with the question of whether I should leave at the earliest opportunity or stay a little longer. Isn't 55 a little early to retire? I knew I would like more time for myself, but did I really need to leave my job to get a little additional time? What was I going to do, where was I going to live, was I really ready to make such a big change in my life? When these are theoretical questions, they are fun and somewhat easy to answer, particularly when you are years away from retirement or the idea of living the rest of your life free to do whatever you desire. But always remember, the degree of difficulty ratchets up as one approaches his own retirement.

I was a retirement manager; I should have had the definitive answer. After much deliberation, I started wondering if maybe there is no such definitive answer. Maybe the selection as to when one retires is a little bit like horseshoes. It doesn't have to be right on the stake; it has to be only close enough. I have never met the person who has been able to answer the question: How much is enough?

As in life or work, a little luck is essential. I was lucky that Janet was motivated several years before my retirement and encouraged me to at least think about and shop for possible locations to consider for retirement. Vacations would turn into real-estate explorations. We would enjoy shopping—the treat of the rich and famous, yet free, providing you don't buy anything! She encouraged me to look for properties somewhere in the South, somewhere not too far from our children, who were living and working in Atlanta, and not so far away as to make us feel isolated.

We started our search within the state of Georgia, but we quickly moved south to Florida. We did however, have one advantage. After living 30 miles from the Canadian border during our early years, we had experienced enough ice and snow to realize we were more heat-tolerant than cold-tolerant.

We struck gold one sunny afternoon. We ran into a gregarious real-estate agent named Howie Molloy. After hellos were exchanged, we said, "Howie, we have only 20 minutes to look. We're on our way back to Atlanta, and it's a work day tomorrow." Howie said, "Twenty minutes is more than enough." It had to be a combination of things—the end of a vacation, the warm sunshine, the sound of the ocean, or the voice of a true believer and his story of the pending dream soon to be developed. Janet was sold immediately; I consented a little later, and I justified the transaction in my own mind by telling myself that she was only asking me to purchase a vacant lot. It was to be in a newly formed subdivision with the promise of sunny weather, beautiful aesthetics, and unlimited activities. For me, the big plus was buying undeveloped property, with the worse-case scenario that it would become investment property with the potential of appreciation. Another upside was the procrastination factor. The longer it took us to decide whether we would ultimately build and relocate to Florida, the more it would continue to work in our favor. It was a little like a savings account, accruing interest as time passed.

I did retire at my earliest opportunity, which in hindsight turned out to be the best decision I could have made, and a new lifestyle started. Our new lifestyle started in the same house, in the same neighborhood, and with the same friends and activities we had throughout our active working life. I didn't envision a need for change, because my friends who I had played golf with were still in the neighborhood, my friends who I rode motorcycles with were still in my neighborhood, and the circle of friends we relied on for all our activities were still in place just a few miles away. Plus, we had lived in Atlanta for more than 15 years. Why should we make a change? We knew we were living in a great city. Yet, our vacant lot in Florida was still there, appreciating in value and serving as an outlet if we ever desired it to become one.

Our new retirement lifestyle started affecting me right away. After 35 years of working at a large company, being surrounded by numerous people every day, and being fully engaged 10 to 12 hours daily, it had gotten into my blood. I didn't miss working 10 to 12 hours a day. What I missed was the interaction of people and life's pace in general. I would wake up in the morning wanting to spend a 10- to 12-hour, fast-paced, exhilarating day, the same as I had been accustomed to. Schedules weren't meshing. I was available; where was everyone else? Just because you retire doesn't mean everyone else is retired. Wouldn't it be nice if all of our friends were the same age and were retiring at the same time? It would be a little bit like high school, when we all had the same schedule and everyone in the class was the same age.

One phrase I kept hearing over and over was "I would like to, but I am so busy, I just can't." Whether it was golf, biking, or grabbing a bite to eat, I kept hearing "It's so crazy over here, I just can't get away." I felt like the person who steps off a fast-moving commuter train: I found myself on the platform with a little extra time on my hands before my next appointment, but everyone else was still on the train, moving as fast as ever, and getting farther away every minute. In reflection, had I not stayed in Atlanta immediately following my retirement, I would have never fully realized that my old working environment, my wonderful Atlanta, wasn't going to coincide with my retiree expectations.

So we decided to build a house on our Florida property. That Florida lot, our savings account, was about to be cashed in. Our backup plan was being executed. We were relocating within a reasonable drive of friends and family, improving on our weather, increasing the number of activities available to us, and placing ourselves in a community with like-minded individuals who were living at a high rate of speed; all I had to do was join the crowd and try to keep up. People here were enjoying similar activities, including golf, exercise, swimming, and tennis.

We have lived here only a short time, but the number of guests and family members who have visited has been a pleasure. I remember once seeing a movie in which the underlying theme was: "If you build it, they will come." Well, we built it, and they are coming. Our daughter's family loves our new location, the grandchildren look forward to visits, our sons think it is wonderful, and our daughter-in-law has plans to visit for the summer already. Our lives have been enriched with the new relationships and friends we have made since our move, and more important, we still carry with us the friendships that we have established over the years and cherish so much.

PART TWO

...

Where do you spend
your newfound time?

STAY BUSY

■ ■ ■

"Do one thing every day that scares you."

–Eleanor Roosevelt

Now is the time to think about the next phase of your life. A 2006 Pew Research Center survey found that expectations and reality differ when predicting the age of retirement. While workers think they'll retire when they are 61, the average age of retirement is actually 57.8 years of age. Today's retirees are generally more affluent, younger, and healthier and can expect to live as many as three decades in their "golden years." In fact, terms such as zoomers (coined by Tim Smart, *U.S. News & World Report*), and the concepts of redirecting, refiring, or reinventing your life after leaving your primary career have all appeared in the media, reflecting the reality that retirement doesn't mean sitting on the sidelines of life.

As noted in Part 1, activities that are challenging and provide a sense of self-worth are one of the keys to a happy retirement. Yes, you can play golf and watch television, but what other options exist? What types of volunteer and lifelong learning opportunities are there? What are some interesting hobbies? Should you start a second (or third or fourth) career?

Time On Your Hands

Will your retirement days be time-filled or time-empty?

To get an idea of how well you'll handle time once you're retired or how well you're presently doing in retirement, take this simple test. For a typical one-week period, estimate in half-hour increments (.5, 1.0, 1.5, etc.) how much time you think you'll spend, or are spending, on the following activities:

Meal preparation _____
Housework, yard work, and maintenance _____
Gardening _____
Exercise (walking, jogging, swimming, aerobics, jazzercise, weight training, etc.) _____
Sporting activities (bicycling, golf, tennis, hiking, canoeing, squash, etc.) _____
Organizational activities (church or civic meetings, socials, religious services) _____
Volunteer work (church, civic, school or special causes) _____

Learning classes of any kind _____

Studying or prep for classes _____

Computer time (e-mail, Web surfing, IM, etc.) _____

Social events (lunch with friends, parties, get-togethers, plays, movies, concerts, entertaining at home, etc.) _____

Hobbies of any kind (not sport-related) _____

Plan/prep for a trip _____

Pet care (walks, grooming, vet visits, playing with pet, etc.) _____

Family visits _____

Reading _____

Shopping _____

Miscellaneous errands (non-shopping) _____

Part-time job _____

Total _____

If male, add 77 (for sleep, eating, and personal hygiene during one week)
If female, add 80.5 (for sleep, eating, and personal hygiene during one week)
Net total _____

Subtract this number from 168 (the number of hours in a week)
Total vacant hours per week _____
For an average day, divide by 7 _____

Reprinted with permission of www.retirementrocket.com

If you were to do the math, you'd realize there are 168 hours a week to fill, which you can do mindlessly or mindfully. Assuming you have the financial wherewithal, ask yourself if there are things you'd like to try or if you want more time to pursue certain interests. If the answer to this question is no, and your spouse or significant other is amenable, keep working. It may be the best thing for you. If the answer is yes, however, the big question then is: How do you reprogram your time?

Should You Stop Working?
Examining the nonfinancial benefits of working can help you decide if you should continue to work at your present job, cut down on the hours you work, change jobs, or perhaps fulfill a passion—volunteer, start your own business, learn a new skill, etc.

Check yes or no for each of the following:
1. Working gives me a sense of accomplishment.
Yes ☐ No ☐
2. I frequently socialize with my colleagues.
Yes ☐ No ☐
3. I like my days to have structure.
Yes ☐ No ☐
4. My feelings about myself are at least partly defined by my work.
Yes ☐ No ☐
5. I get more satisfaction from work than leisure.
Yes ☐ No ☐

6. I look forward to going to work.
Yes ☐ No ☐

7. The pros of my job outweigh the cons.
Yes ☐ No ☐

8. I can't think of many other things I'd rather be doing than going to work.
Yes ☐ No ☐

9. There is a dream job I've always wanted to pursue.
Yes ☐ No ☐

10. It's easier to continue working than to organize each day myself.
Yes ☐ No ☐

How many times did you answer "Yes"? If at least half of your answers are in the affirmative, work provides significant psychological benefits that will need to be replaced by other activities if you stop working.

PERSONALITY AND GOAL-SETTING

Are you a planner? One of the authors (Jan) has her next four years of vacations planned out, knows the next five books she is going to read, and looks at *TV Guide* for the coming week to see if there are any programs she'll need to tape because of conflicting commitments. Cathy, on the other hand, lives mainly in the moment, picks up and goes on trips (without hotel reservations) at the drop of a hat, signs up for a cooking class or tennis round-robin at the last minute, and jumps in to volunteer for a worthy cause without any hesitation. Although they have different personalities and vastly different methods, Jan and Cathy have one thing in common: They both have goals they want to accomplish.

In order to have a successful retirement, you'll want to set goals. Otherwise, rather than enjoying leisure activities, you'll really just be experiencing idleness, and the research shows that people who aren't engaged in purposeful activities are generally not as happy as those who are. Whether you're talking about starting a new business, taking up birding, becoming a mentor, or trying out for a community theater production, it's best to be flexible, try out new things, have a natural curiosity about life, and have some kind of plan for your future. So regardless of your individual personality traits, how do you go about setting goals?

First, take the time to decide what you'd like to accomplish, and make lists. If you are part of a couple, set down both individual and joint ideas relating to work, leisure activities, health, lifelong learning, relationships, or any other area. Recognize that each person in the relationship has valid needs and wants. Decide which are interests you share, and realize having time apart for separate interests is also important. Brainstorm all possibilities, then evaluate and prune the unworkable ones.

Now comes the fun part. Take your list, pick three items on it, and turn them into goals. Here's how:

- Turn each item into a specific, positive
  statement. For example, "I don't want to be

intellectually stagnant" doesn't cut it. "I want to take a European history course at the local community college during the fall semester" does.

- Make your goals achievable within a defined time period. If you know you're scheduled for hernia surgery on October 1, you may want to rethink whether you can complete a fall semester history course. You want to dream, yet still be realistic.
- Remind yourself of your goals. Writing them out and placing them in a visible spot will help reinforce them.

Some people already know the goals they wish to attain, while others may want to consider some possibilities in the areas of education, hobbies, volunteering, the world of work, and travel (which is such a big area, we've given it a section by itself). And still others, well, they could use a little help deciding. If this sounds like you, keep reading.

> **SMART.** This easy-to-remember acronym describes the characteristics of goal-setting: Specific, Measurable, Attainable, Realistic, and Time-sensitive.

LIFELONG LEARNING

Remember the three Rs? There are more opportunities than ever for the mature learner to complete a degree, go back to school for professional reasons, pursue classes for enrichment, to increase social contacts, or just for the fun of it. In some cases, you don't even have to "go back." If you have a computer and an internet connection, you can curl up with a cup of coffee in your favorite robe and slippers and take a course online! About a third of all adults are enrolled in some type of formal education, according to the Department of Education.

DEGREE PROGRAMS

The majority of adult students (about 70 percent) enroll in higher education to attain a degree. Most are seeking bachelor's degrees, some are working on master's degrees or doctorate degrees, and others are after associate's degrees. The reasons vary: finishing a degree that was interrupted years ago by family or work constraints, working on professional development, achieving a goal for which they now have the time and financial resources, or training for a new career.

If pursuing a degree is a path you want to consider, keep in mind that many colleges and universities will exempt you from entrance exams such as the SAT and ACT if you're over a certain age. If you're thinking of advanced degrees in medicine or law, however, you will need to take the MCAT or LSAT. When applying to a college, you'll probably have to provide any previous transcripts you have, which will be assessed by the college counselor to determine which credits you already possess that may be applied toward your degree. You may also be able to receive credit by taking the CLEP (College-Level Examination Program) test, a credit-by-exam program that tests your knowledge of undergraduate subjects (www.collegeboard.com/clep). There are almost 3,000 colleges in the country that give credit and/or advanced standing for successful completion of CLEP exams.

If finances are a concern, there are several avenues to explore. Many colleges and universities offer classes at free or reduced tuition rates to mature learners. Community colleges often offer particularly attractive incentives. For example, at Kankakee Community College in Illinois, students 60 and older can enroll in credit courses without any tuition charges, provided there are enough paying students to cover the cost of the course. Check out the deals at the college or university near you. You may also be eligible for tax breaks, such as the Hope Tax Credit or a Lifetime Learning Credit (call the IRS Help Desk at 800-876-1715 or visit www.irs.gov and read Tax Topic 605: Education Credits or IRS Publication 970: Tax Benefits for Higher Education). Consider tapping into your IRA (without a tax penalty) for approved educational needs. College, federal, and state loans and grants are available, as well as scholarships. Meet with a financial-aid officer at the colleges you are considering, and check out the Free Application for Federal Student Aid (FAFSA) at www.fafsa.ed.gov, Sallie Mae (www.salliemae.com), Free Scholarship Search (www.freschinfo.com), and Fast Web (www.fastweb.com). If you're female, the Business and Professional Women's Foundation offers scholarships if you meet certain criteria (www.bpwusa.org or 202-293-1100), and the American Association of University Women Education Foundation offers fellowships, grants, and awards (www.aauw.org or 800-785-7700).

The term "college senior" can have a whole new meaning.

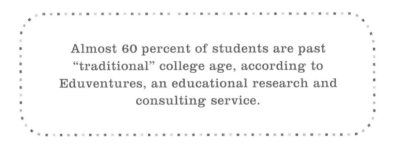

Almost 60 percent of students are past "traditional" college age, according to Eduventures, an educational research and consulting service.

DISTANCE LEARNING

If you've always wanted to conquer calculus, but fear you'll be in a class of young adults desperately competing to get into medical school—or if taking a class while sipping coffee in your robe and slippers appeals to you—distance learning is the way to go.

Distance learning, also called distance education, is found in a variety of formats. There are classes offered in "real time," classes that you can take on your own schedule, classes where you never meet in person, and classes in which some actual face-to-face interactions are required. Entire degrees (from a bachelor's to a doctorate), certificate courses, credit and noncredit classes, continuing education courses, and courses for professional development are all possibilities with distance learning. Delivery of class materials can be via the Internet, video conferencing, satellite, cable TV, and so on.

If you're looking to take classes toward a degree, or transfer credit classes to another institution, it's imperative that you choose your distance-learning classes from an accredited institution, and if you want your credits to transfer, check to see whether the receiving college will accept your distance-education credits. To be honest, the perception of diploma mills dies hard. Surveys show about one out of three employers looks somewhat askance at a distance-education degree. So before signing up for credit courses, do your homework. Visit www.distancelearn.about.com for a wealth of information on distance learning, accredited institutions, free online courses, financial information, and the like. Another site, www.classesusa.com, also contains information related to distance education.

People who do best with this type of instruction are self-starters who like to work independently, have good time-management skills, are goal oriented, and feel comfortable using technology as a teaching tool. If you know you'd miss the interaction of spirited discussions and immediate feedback from professors and fellow students, distance learning wouldn't be the right choice for you. In fact, distance-learning courses have a dropout rate about 20 percent higher than do brick and mortar courses.

Cost varies widely. For example, at the University of Phoenix, a major accredited player in distance education, about 100,000 students "attend" online undergraduate, graduate, and doctoral programs. The cost per credit for an undergraduate course is about $500; for a graduate course, about $600; and for a doctoral course, about $700. You can register for unlimited 30-day access to one course for $9.95 or for a year's unlimited access to personal and business classes for $99.99 through QuickKnowledge (www. quicknowledge.com or 888-606-0004). If you don't want to pay at all, ThirdAge (www.thirdage.com) offers free online workshops, such as "Get Ready to Invest" or "Master Your Sex Life." SeniorNet (www.seniornet.org) offers free tutorials, guides, and discussion-based courses as well.

The world of education is literally at your fingertips.

ADULT EDUCATION

Although adult education courses can be taken in the distance format, let's turn our attention to taking courses in an actual classroom setting but without worrying about credits, degrees, or transferability.

As mentioned before, many institutions of higher learning give breaks to mature learners. At Florida's state universities, for example, tuition is waived for adults age 60 and older if there is space available, they meet Florida residency requirements, and classes are not taken for credit. State colleges and universities in Texas allow seniors (65 and older) to take up to six free hours of credit or noncredit courses per semester or summer term, if space allows. Of course, credit-free also means exam-free, homework-free, and term paper-free! Great deals are out there. Contact the local colleges to see about their individual tuition policies.

If you're more interested in a residential program (but not a dorm!), look into Senior Summer School (www.seniorsummerschool.com or 800-847-2466). You can take a two-week current events class offered by San Diego State University for an all-inclusive (sans transportation) price of $1,600. Elderhostel (www.elderhostel.org) combines education and travel. How about the 12-day "Birding: The Hot Spots of Costa Rica" offering for about $1,900? Sign us up!

If you'd rather stay closer to home and are interested in learning for its own sake, many noncredit adult-education classes, community classes, and enrichment classes exist. One member-driven organization of adult learners, the Osher Lifelong Learning Institute (www.

osherfoundation.org), is represented on campuses in about 40 states and in Canada. For example, the University of South Carolina (Beaufort) charges a $25 annual membership fee and registration fees ranging from $4 to $60 per term. You may then take as many courses during each term as you'd like. You can take peer-taught courses in areas such as language, political issues, science, and literature.

With all the options available, lifelong learning can easily become a reality.

Grandma Moses (Anna Mary Robertson Moses) began painting in her late seventies and continued painting for more than 20 years.

HOBBIES

Winston Churchill once said, "Broadly speaking, human beings can be divided into three classes: those who are toiled to death, those who are worried to death, and those who are bored to death." To be sure you don't fall into the third category, consider some hobbies as you reprogram your time. A hobby enriches your life by increasing your knowledge, sharpening your skills, and/or bringing you inner peace.

You may already be an avid golfer, tennis player, reader, oenophile (wine lover), or philatelist (stamp collector). There are an endless variety of hobbies out there; the second stage of your life is a perfect opportunity to hone old hobbies and explore new ones. Here are some examples.

Genealogy. If you want to find out more about your ancestors, there are dozens of books written on the subject, courses you can take, and the treasure trove that is the Internet. (Check out the resources listing for this chapter for a few suggestions.)

Dance. Exotic, salsa, line, ballroom, square, swing . . . you get the idea. Some of these don't even require a partner—just show up.

Photography. With digital cameras, you can now zip your creations to far-flung relatives with the press of a button.

Reading. After relocating to Bellingham, Washington, Melanie F. began a book club that meets every 6 weeks. Members alternate picking books and hosting the meetings in their homes. She not only met more people and expanded her social-support group, but she's reading a heck of a lot of good literature. Many books now contain discussion guides because of the booming popularity of reading clubs. Your local library or bookstore can give you information about setting up book clubs as well as recommend lists. (The bookstore where Melanie's club members purchase their books gives them a 10 percent discount.) Or you can access a site such as www.bookbrowse.com. If you don't want to leave your home, you can join an online book club; for a few possibilities, browse www.book-clubs-resource.com.

Exercise/sports. Improving your body as well as your mind is certainly a noble endeavor. Your local health club, YMCA/YWCA, community center, or medical center may offer fitness programs or facilities, from aerobics and swimming to weights and yoga. Sign up with a personal trainer for a few classes to get started on the right track, or lace up those sneakers and start walking. Consider taking up a new sport. So many baby boomers have taken up snowboarding that they've been called "grays on trays." What about bowling? Nancy and Jeff S. recently moved to northeast Florida and invited some new friends and acquaintances to bowl once a week. Sixteen people now meet at Coquina Lanes every Thursday at 4:00. They've named themselves the "Alley Oops."

Acting. If you've been longing to perform under the bright lights, consider joining an acting troupe. Helene G. lives in Leisure World in Silver Spring, Maryland, and snagged a role as Anna in *The King* *and I* through Leisure World's Fun and Fancy Theatre Group. If you don't want to be onstage, consider a behind-the-scenes role such as helping with makeup, lighting, costumes, scenery, or publicity. If you are uncertain where to look, call the theater department of your local college or university and ask for suggestions, or look under "theaters" in the Yellow Pages. In 1999, there were 79 senior performing groups in the United States. This number has mushroomed to about 600 today.

Birding. The U.S. Forest Service reports that the quickest growing outdoor activity in the United States is birding. With 10,000 bird species, enjoyment of nature, and the social aspect of being in a group, this is a great hobby. A few good sites include: www.birding.com, www.birder.com, www.audubon.org, and www.birdwatching.com. As this last Web site states, enjoy "your lifetime ticket to the theater of nature."

Games. "Use it or lose it" is an adage frequently invoked in relation to keeping our brains energized. Research has shown people who stay cerebrally challenged tend to lead richer, fuller lives and may even stave off diseases such as Alzheimer's. Jason R. and his wife, Beverly, arrange a monthly game night with four other couples. They usually alternate among Pictionary, Trivial Pursuit, Outburst, Charades, and card games and enjoy the social interaction as much as the intellectual stimulation. On a more solitary note, you can enjoy crossword puzzles, sudoku, acrostics, and jigsaw puzzles. Try www.upuzzles.com or www.queendom.com (click on "mind stretchers") for a good selection, or the hot Nintendo game *Brain Age*, which was designed by a neuroscientist.

VOLUNTEERING

If you find that classes, working, hobbies, and/or travel aren't enough to give you a feeling of satisfaction and fulfillment, consider Winston Churchill's words: "We make a living by what we get; we make a life by what we give."

More than one in three American adults volunteered in 2005, averaging about 50 hours per year, according to the federal government. The study found that women donate their time more than men. Utah has the most volunteers (50 percent of its residents) and Nevada the fewest (19 percent). Although by no means all-inclusive, here's an A-to-Z list of volunteer opportunities.

Adult literacy. One in four adults in America struggles with literacy issues. To address this crisis, Proliteracy Worldwide (www.proliteracy.org or 888-528-2224) is attempting to recruit 100,000 volunteers.

Big Brothers/Big Sisters. According to the organization, the only requirements are a willingness to make a new friend and a desire to share some fun with a young person. Contact www.bbbs.org or check the Yellow Pages for a local agency.

Community policing/patrols. Contact your local police department or the Office of Community Oriented Policing Services (COPS) at www.cops.usdoj.gov.

Disaster response. The workforce of the American Red Cross is 97 percent volunteers! This organization provides training, if necessary. Go online to www.red cross.org (click "volunteer") or call your local Red Cross unit or the National Headquarters at 800-733-2767.

Elimination of substandard housing. Habitat for Humanity is working in more than 80 countries to build affordable housing for people in need. Visit www.habitat.org, call the affiliate nearest you, or contact their Partner Service Center at 229-924-6935.

Food for the homebound. Bring food to people who are disabled or homebound through Meals on Wheels. More than one million nutritious meals are served every day through churches, charities, and citizen and community groups. Find a provider in your area, or contact the Meals on Wheels Association of America at www.mowaa.org or 703-548-5558.

Guardian ad litem or court-appointed special advocate work. Represent neglected and abused children during judicial proceedings. Contact CASA (Court Appointed Special Advocates for Children) at www.nationalcasa.org or 800-628-3233.

Hospice care. Bring dignity and comfort to the terminally ill and their families. "Hospice is not a place but a concept of care." Contact the Hospice Foundation of America (www.hospicefoundation.org or 800-854-3402).

Income-tax preparation. Be one of more than 32,000 volunteer tax aides through the AARP Foundation. Contact www.aarp.org/taxaide or call 888-227-7669.

Job assistance. Dress for Success helps low-income women enter the workforce through the donation of work and interview-appropriate clothing. Or donate your time as a personal shopper, office helper, or clothes sorter for this global organization. Contact www.dressforsuccess.org and click on "locations" for the closest affiliate, or call 212-532-1922.

K.E.E N. (Kids Enjoy Exercise Now). Pair up with a mentally or physically challenged child or young adult and participate in recreational activities. Check out www.keenusa.org or call 866-903-5336.

Library work. Be a greeter, give tours, assist in clerical work, help introduce patrons to electronic resources, shelve books, prepare children's programs, index newspapers, and so on. Call your local library for available positions.

Mentoring. Help a young person improve his or her life by being there and providing a good example. Many companies, churches, and civic groups sponsor mentoring programs. Or contact the National Mentoring Partnership at www.mentoring.org, where you can enter your zip code and find a list of local organizations that provide mentoring or call 703-224-2200.

Nurturing. Join the Foster Grandparent Program and help children and teens with special or exceptional needs. There are several requirements to be a foster grandparent relating to your age, time commitment, and training. Foster Grandparents receive a modest stipend if income-eligible. For more information, contact www.seniorcorps.org or call 800-424-8867.

Offering assistance to the elderly and homebound. Join the Senior Companion Program and help those in need with transportation to appointments, shopping, and other helpful chores. Senior companions receive reimbursement for some costs and service-related accident and liability insurance. The Senior Companion Program can be accessed through www.seniorcorps. org or 800-424-8867.

Providing help for the homeless. On any given night, almost a million people will be homeless. Churches, companies, and many civic organizations aid the homeless, or you can contact the National Law Center on Homelessness and Poverty, whose goal is to help prevent and end homelessness. They can be reached at www.nlchp.org or 202-638-2535.

Quilting. If you like to sew, you can provide new, homemade blankets or quilts to ill or traumatized children from birth to 18 years of age through the 100 percent volunteer Linus Project (www.projectlinus.org or 309-664-7814), or make a quilt/sleeping bag for a homeless person (www.reese.org/sharon/uglyqult.htm or 717-289-4335).

Reading. Read to children in clinic waiting rooms through Reach Out and Read (www.reachoutandread. org or 617-629-8042) or Recording for the Blind and Dyslexic (www.rfbd.org or 866-732-3585).

Special Olympics work. Join more than 700,000 Special Olympics volunteers at the local, state, national, or international level. Contact www.special-olympics.org or call 202-628-3630.

Tutoring. Go through a community or faith-based organization to tutor children or adults, or contact VolunteerMatch at www.volunteermatch.org or 415-241-6868 for opportunities near you.

Ushering. If you want to enjoy operas or plays as well as contribute to the art world, consider volunteering to be an usher. Generally, theaters prefer a commitment on a regular basis, and of course you'll need to arrive early, be helpful and courteous, dress the part, and be able to assist those who need it. Contact your local performing-arts center.

Voter registration. The voter turnout since 1972 has remained virtually unchanged. Help get the vote out! Contact your Board of Elections to become a voter registration volunteer.

Walking a shelter dog. Contact your local Humane Society, Animal Shelter League, or ASPCA. Get exercise while you do a good deed!

Xenophon Therapeutic Riding Center. Sign up to help with therapeutic riding lessons for disabled children and adults. You may groom the horses, provide lessons, or work on landscaping or repairs. For a list of additional therapeutic riding centers, go to www.narha.org and click on "Find a Center."

Your chance to make a difference. Here's the catchall category. Think of what you can do to give back. For example, the fourth Saturday of every October has been designated "Make a Difference Day" by USA Weekend magazine. To get involved with this initiative, go to www.usaweekend.com and click on "Make a Difference Day." The site has an idea generator to help you formulate a project as well as register a project. Or, think locally. Which of your friends, neighbors, or relatives could use a hand with his or her household or yard chores, grocery shopping, or babysitting? Offer your services; people often feel uncomfortable asking for help.

Zoo work. What's doing at the zoo for volunteers? Interpret exhibits, help maintain the grounds, care for baby animals, assist with promotional events, be a docent, help the keepers feed the animals, or clean and maintain animal exhibits.

If that list isn't enough, here are some additional organizations that list numerous opportunities to volunteer.

More than 35 million Americans over 50 belong to AARP, an organization that "is dedicated to enhancing quality of life for all as we age." Put "volunteer" in the search bar at www.aarp.org or call 888-687-2277.

Network for Good (www.networkforgood.org) was founded by the AOL, Cisco Systems, and Yahoo!. This site allows you to volunteer and/or donate money.

Points of Light Foundation, founded by President George H. W. Bush in 1990, works with the Volunteer Center National Network to help bring solutions to community problems. Contact the foundation at www.pointsoflight.org or 800-750-7653.

VolunteerMatch helps you to search for volunteer opportunities (almost 40,000 of them!) by zip code or type of organization. Contact them at www.volunteer match.org or 415-241-6868.

Volunteers of America has faith-based programs that work to rehabilitate people, not just treat their symptoms. Their outreach includes correction facilities, schools, churches, and social-service and law-enforcement agencies. Offices are community based, so find one near you, go to www.volunteersofamerica.org, or call the national office at 202-729-8000.

STAYING IN THE GAME

Will you learn, then earn, and then return? According to the 2006 "Retirement Confidence Survey," sponsored by the Employee Benefit Research Institute (EBRI), 77 percent of boomers plan to work full or part time after leaving their primary careers, or alternate work and leisure time before retiring completely. Finances are the biggest reason for working, but enjoyment of work and being enticed by the idea of doing something different career-wise are also factors.

Let's take a look at the financial aspects of work first. The EBRI found that 68 percent of current workers (including their spouses) had less than $50,000 socked away for retirement, and almost 60 percent reported that they didn't expect to receive any health insurance from their employers.

Assume that you don't have to work for financial reasons. Should you still work? The nonfinancial rewards of work can be just as compelling. As described earlier, these include a sense of identity, status, intellectual engagement, social interaction, structure, and feelings of pride and accomplishment. Recall that in the Cornell Retirement and Well-Being Study, referred to in Part 1, the major reason for retiring for both men and women was "to do other things." If there aren't other things you'd rather be doing, by all means, keep working as long as you can (if you have a significant other who's okay with it).

Of course, work options don't have to be all or nothing—full time or no time. You can work part time or part of the year, consult on a freelance basis, transition to a new career, or start your own business.

Let's say you want to work, for whatever reason, but also wish to change gears. What are some of the realities and options of staying in the workforce or reentering it after leaving a primary career?

AGEISM

Does age discrimination exist? Not legally. The federal Age Discrimination in Employment Act (ADEA), passed in 1967, states, "It shall be unlawful for an employer to fail or refuse to hire or to discharge any individual or otherwise discriminate against any individual with respect to his compensation, terms, conditions, or privileges of employment, because of such individual's age."

There can be a gap between legality and reality, however. During 2005, the Equal Employment Opportunity Commission (EEOC) received 5,088 age-discrimination complaints, the average job search was 17.8 weeks for people under 55 years old, but 24.1 weeks for those over 55, and Texas A&M Economics professor Joanna Lahey found that companies were more than 40 percent more likely to interview a younger job seeker rather than an older job seeker.

Unfortunately, some employers feel that older workers are more set in their ways, have less energy and more health problems, aren't as technologically savvy, require higher salaries, and won't work as hard or long as younger workers. Historically, the implicit agreement was that an employee would stay with one company throughout his or her work career, starting out at lower wages, but progressing to higher wages as he or she became older. This paradigm is no longer true. With people routinely changing jobs every several years, and younger workers wanting higher wages when they come on board, the old way is no longer the model.

Most experts are upbeat about the future of older workers, however. With baby boomers retiring from primary careers (more than 76 million), and fewer younger workers to replace them (48 million Gen X employees), labor shortages will force companies to retain, retrain (if necessary), and value the older employee. For many employers, the bottom line will be whether the employee meets their company's needs; the experience, work ethic, and maturity of boomers will become valuable commodities.

The distinction of oldest employee goes to F. Waldo McBurney, 104, a Kansas beekeeper and author of *My First 100 Years!*

JOB-HUNTING SUGGESTIONS

First, consider what's important to you. Is the amount of money crucial, or is flexibility, novelty, helping others, or using your strengths just as high a priority? Will you need additional formal education? Are you willing to make trade-offs? A career counselor or career coach can help crystallize and focus your priorities and narrow your job search. For assistance from one, contact the National Board for Certified Counselors and Affiliates (www.nbcc.org or 336-547-0607) or the Coach Connection (www.findyourcoach.com or 800-887-7214), or join a group such as the Five O'Clock Club (www.fiveoclockclub.com or 800-538-6645), which assists in job searches.

You can also take self-tests to help you determine where your interests lie. Free self-assessments are available at www.careergames.com. This site also gives tips on interviewing, negotiating, and answering difficult interview questions.

Let friends, former colleagues, members of groups or professional associations you belong to, and acquaintances know you are looking for work—and what type of work you desire (about 35 percent of people are hired through networking). Volunteer in an area you are interested in, or work at a temporary staffing service to "try out" different work paths. (Adecco, www.usadecco.com, is one such company.) Not only will you find out if you're interested in the field, but you'll be ready and willing if the company decides to hire. Use newspapers or online search engines such as Monster.com and HotJobs.com (although only about

7 percent of jobs are filled through Internet sites, according to the *Wall Street Journal* Executive Career Site). You can also go online to sites geared toward workers 50 and older, such as Seniors4Hire (www.seniors4hire.org or 714-848-0996) or Senior Job Bank (www.seniorjobbank.org or 888-501-0804).

If you have a particular area of expertise, look for Web sites that reflect your background and have job postings. For example, Mary S. relocated to New Jersey after a divorce and wanted to continue in her profession as a media specialist in an elementary school. She went to Rutger's University Web site and found media specialist positions that required her specific credentials, as well as openings in the area where she was relocating. Also, don't overlook small companies!

To find out where the jobs are (and hence, where the demand is), check out the U.S. Department of Labor's Occupational Outlook Handbook, which is revised every other year; it contains a treasure trove of information about growth projections, wages, education, and working conditions for specific careers. Predicted areas of highest employment growth until 2014 include healthcare (no big surprise as we boomers advance in age), employment services, technical (think computer) services, the leisure and hospitality industry (all the boomers are ready to spend their money!), and the financial-services industries. If these areas appeal to you, you're in luck! Click on www.bls.gov/oco to access the newest edition of the handbook online.

You'll also have to update (or dust off) your résumé.

Don't feel obligated to list every job you've ever had; concentrate on those positions that are pertinent to the employment you are seeking. If you're looking to change careers, or if you're reentering the workforce after a hiatus, concentrate on the transferable skills applicable to the new position, and downplay job titles if necessary.

Emphasize your accomplishments, results, and outstanding qualifications in a succinct paragraph at the top of your résumé. Include any computer expertise, coursework, or professional development to accentuate your openness to learning, as well as your e-mail address. When e-mailing a résumé, don't send it as an attachment in case it can't (or won't) be opened, and e-mail a copy to yourself prior to sending it to a potential employer to make sure it looks like you want it to look. In your cover letter, emphasize that you are a proven entity (don't say you've worked for 30 years) and that you are flexible, adaptable, and willing to learn, and that you have transferable skills.

There is some disagreement as to what type of résumé older workers should use. A functional résumé highlights accomplishments and talents and downplays when the work was done. But many employers and recruiters know this type of résumé can be hiding work gaps and age, and dislike them. Chronological résumés are the preferred choice among most of those in hiring positions, but they can be a disadvantage if your latest experience doesn't match the new position, or if age matters. Combining both types into a "chrono-functional" résumé could be the best bet. An excellent site for résumé types, sample résumés, and tips on negotiating and networking can be found at www.careerjournal.com. Click on "Job-Hunting Advice."

Once your foot is in the door—you have the interview—again emphasize your flexibility, motivation, interpersonal skills, and willingness to learn. Let them know you want to contribute to the company and that you're not looking for a job because you're broke! Use your age to your advantage, stressing your experience with problem solving, a proven track record, and strong work ethic. If you're happy to work part-time, let the prospective employer know you are a bargain. You have tons of experience, but you don't have to be paid what they might pay a younger, full-time employee. Slip in (assuming it's true) how you're still playing tennis or love to downhill ski, hike, or swim to convey that you are a vital, energetic person. Address any questions (insidious or obvious) about your age forthrightly by reassuring the interviewer you can handle the job as well as bring experience, enthusiasm, and wisdom to the position. If asked how you feel about working for someone younger than you, AARP suggests you respond, "When I get to the point where I can't learn from someone younger or older than I, I will stop working." Be sure you're knowledgeable about the company, and follow up with a handwritten thank-you note.

> The Bureau of Labor Statistics estimates that by 2010 approximately 33 percent of the labor force will be comprised of "mature" workers (those over 45).

NEW CAREERS

Don't sell yourself short! There are jobs to consider besides the usual greeter, retailer, cashier, food preparer, and server positions. Here are just a few possibilities to ponder if you'd like to embark on a new direction.

Health-care worker. For careers in demand, look to the health-care industry and consider diploma courses to become a home-health aide, medical assistant, pharmacy technologist, nurse aide, EKG technologist, or physical-therapy aide. These are relatively short courses (weeks or months), relatively low cost (usually under $1,000), and many employers will reimburse your tuition costs if you work for them. There are 2-year associate of arts or associate of science degrees in such areas as medical transcription or respiratory therapy. Look to your local community college or technical school for more information. If you have the time, energy, and money, look into pharmacy school. There is a huge demand for pharmacists, and the pay is excellent.

Captioner. A captioner converts the spoken word to text. Hearing-impaired students, television broadcasts, conventions, stockholder meetings, and court proceedings may all use the services of a captioner. There is an increased need for captioners due to mandatory closed captioning for 95 percent of all new television programs. Captioning can be done on-site or off-site, in real time or not. If you are working as an independent contractor, there are costs for the necessary equipment (around $15,000). Salaries average about $50,000, but can get into the six figures. For a list of programs and career paths, contact the National Court Reporters Association at www.ncraonline.org or call 800-272-6272.

Seasonal work. If you love the great outdoors, consider working at a national park, ski resort, ranch, theme park, tour company, on a ship, etc. For a seasonal commitment, you can receive lodging, meals, and a paycheck. It won't be the Ritz, and you won't make a fortune,but it may be the right thing if you're open to new experiences and like to work hard. For more information, contact www.coolworks.com—there is even a link for the "older and bolder"—or call 406-848-2380. Check out Xanterra Parks and Resorts (www.xanterra. com or 303-600-3400) if you're interested in managing the concessions (lodging, food, gift shops, etc.) at national or state parks or resorts.

Bank teller. If you like detail, you may want to pursue this position, which handles the routine operations of a bank. About 25 percent of bank tellers work part-time.

Customer-service representative. These employees serve as the liaison between the public and their companies. Most are employed by financial, communication, and insurance institutions. The U.S. Department of Labor predicts that employment of customer-service representatives will increase faster than the average through 2010. Maybe by then we won't always get a recording when we call a company! Or consider working from home. Although it seems that scams abound in this category (stuffing envelopes, anyone?), there is a definite legitimate side to this industry. "Homeshoring" allows customer-service agents to work out of their homes, primarily in phone work and data entry. Some people hired for this type of work are independent contractors; others are employees of the company. Examples of firms that hire stay-at-home customer-service reps include: Working Solutions (www.workingsolutions.com), West Corporation (www.workathomeagent.com), LiveOps (www.liveops.com), and Alpine Access (www.alpineaccess.com). Pay ranges from $6 to $20 an hour, and there are certain home setup requirements.

Nursing-home feeding assistant. A new federal regulation allows people to be feeding assistants in nursing homes after an eight-hour training course. Previously, you had to be a nursing assistant, with at least 75 hours of training. The rule pertains to nursing homes that accept Medicare or Medicaid. Contact nursing homes near you for more information.

Tour guide. Escort groups or individuals through museums, important buildings, parks, and the like.

For example, Tourmobile Sightseeing in Washington, DC, provides narrated shuttle tours to the historic sites in Washington and Virginia. Contact the attractions you are interested in and see if they hire and train tour guides.

Mystery shopper. According to Service Intelligence, a mystery shopping company, secret shoppers "anonymously observe and document the quality of service at a store or business on a given day. Clients can then evaluate a sample of service delivery, product knowledge, and facility maintenance at corporate stores or franchises." Retail, health care, banking, finance, and fast-food restaurants are examples of where you could be a mystery shopper. Pay is about $10 to $25 per hour. Contact Service Intelligence (www.experienceexchange.com or 678-513-4776) or Mystery Shoppers (www.mystery-shoppers.com or 800-424-0871).

Focus-group member or survey subject. Who doesn't like to give their opinion? And what's better than giving it and being paid for it? Participating in surveys or focus groups can result in gifts or extra cash and is a fun way to spend a few hours. One of the authors served in a focus group after being approached by an employee of a consumer-research group in a fast-food restaurant. Two weeks later, for about two hours, ten of us met in a conference room in an office building and were questioned on our eating habits, amounts we spent on meals, how often we ate out, and our favorite kinds of food, while researchers behind one-way mirrors were taking notes (they informed us of this). When the pleasant discussion, accompanied by snacks, was over, we were each handed $60 in cash. To find a research company near you, access the New York American Marketing Association's Greenbook (www.greenbook.org) and search their national directory by desired location, or look for ads in local or college newspapers. Earn cash or prizes over the Internet at www.buzzback.com. Whether you are asked to participate in a survey is a function of the demographics a company needs.

Bed-and-breakfast owner. What about using your home or purchasing a place for a B and B? Some retirees go this route, but be sure to consider some of the issues involved: The location must be desirable, the place you plan to use must be zoned for a B and B, and you'll need to obtain insurance. Gross annual income for an average-size bed and breakfast is around $60,000. If interested, visit some B and Bs and take a seminar about owning and operating one. You can take online courses at www.seminars-on-line.com, which run from $60 to $200, depending on content and length, of course.

Job-sharer. Consider taking a full-time position and sharing it with a coworker. Robert T., for example, taught high school biology for many years but wanted to scale back and have his afternoons free for golf and volunteer work. He was able to work out a deal with a new mother, Cay S., who also wanted to return to teaching science, but on a part-time basis. So they shared the full-time science position, prorating their benefits (sometimes one person is covered by a spouse or has other arrangements and may be able to forgo all or some of the benefits). If you're interested in this type of position, and you have a willing coworker, submit a proposal to your employer outlining the concept of job-sharing, how the position would be structured, and what the benefits are to the employer.

Teacher of English as a second or foreign language (ESL/EFL). If you'd like to combine work and travel, consider teaching English in a foreign country or at one of many locations within the United States. Many positions require a college degree; some require a TEFL (Teaching English as a Foreign Language) certificate, which can be obtained in the United States. TESOL (Teachers of English to Speakers of Other Languages (www.tesol.org or 888-547-3369) gives locations of courses and answers many questions about pursuing this career). ESL Teacher's Board (www.eslteachersboard.com) lists positions and descriptions for ESL teachers. For example, a one-year contract teaching in China (Guangzhou) with a TESOL or equivalent certification is advertised with a salary of about $2,500 per month.

Club Med staffer. No, you don't have to be a hardbody to apply for a position with Club Med, and about 90 positions are available, from accountant to windsurfing instructor. See www.clubmedjobs.com for more specifics.

Work on a cruise ship. Contact each cruise line separately for a listing of available positions. Some Web sites charge a fee for this service. For a list of cruise lines, go to www.raynorshyn.com, and click on

"Official Cruise Line Links." For men only (who like to dance): You can be a gentleman host on a cruise ship www.theworkingvacation.com.

Realtor. Real estate attracts those who are people-oriented, flexible, realize that there won't be a steady paycheck, and don't wish to have a nine-to-five job. You'll need to take the appropriate real-estate course, pass the licensing exam, and be sponsored by a broker or real-estate company in the state in which you wish to be licensed. Contact the Board of Realtors in the location where you wish to be licensed to find out the specifics.

Trucker. "Get your motor running. . ." The American Trucking Association estimates that there is a need for 540,000 truckers a year, particularly long-haul heavy-duty truck drivers. Average weekly pay in 2004 was $682, and this is expected to rise with a shortage of truckers. Background checks, an English language requirement, a commercial driver's license (CDL), and training if you're an entry-level CDL driver are usually necessary for employment.

> Try out a new career. Vocation Vacations (www.vocationvacations.com or 866-888-6329) allows you to "test drive your dream job." Actor, alpaca farmer, wine-bar owner, jewelry designer . . . the list is exhaustive, and you pay a fee to be mentored by a pro in your area of interest.

STARTING YOUR OWN BUSINESS

The dream of some retirees is to take a passion or hobby and turn it into a money-making venture, whether it's painting, writing, opening a restaurant or boutique, or having a consulting business. Although 16 percent of workers over 50 are self-employed, the reality is that about half of businesses fail within the first four years. Here are a few things to think about if you're contemplating starting your own business.

Money. Cash-flow problems are the biggest contributor to small-business failures. Look into sources of outside money, rather than funding your business with personal savings. A business plan that includes all the financial information should be reviewed by an accountant or financial planner and should also define your niche market.

Personality. You need perseverance, since the time to plan and turn a profit can take a few years; the ability to cope with rejection, since you are likely to experience some; the stamina to start a new venture; and the desire and energy to solicit business. Think about why you are pursuing the goal of having your own business: Are you bored? Looking for a new life experience? Using it as an escape from dealing with other issues? Do you want to make money? Or is it a combination of factors?

Sole proprietorship, joint enterprise, or franchise. Consider whether you'd like a partner to share the work as well as the profits, or decide if a franchise is a possibility for you. Investments in franchises can range from under $15,000 to $400,000 or more. Check out www.franchisedirect.com or www.franchise.com for more information.

Will it be "everyone back in the (labor) pool"? Some will be pushed in, some will tentatively test the water, some will jump in wholeheartedly, and some will avoid the (labor) pool like hydrophobes.

In summary, instead of retirement being about what you're not doing (working, raising a family, rushing from one commitment to another), make it about what you are doing (letting your creative juices flow, learning new things, rediscovering yourself and those you love, giving back, and "smelling the roses"). As George Lorimer, editor of the *Saturday Evening Post,* said, "You've got to get up every morning with determination if you're going to go to bed with satisfaction." It's really never too late to start something new. Golda Meir was first elected prime minister of Israel at 71!

TRAVEL

Dreaming about that once-in-a-lifetime South Seas vacation? Considering comforting children in an orphanage in Yaroslavl, Russia? Single and interested in travel? Disabled but wish to take a trip? Longing to meet emperor penguins in Antarctica nose to beak? Want an educational vacation, or looking for a place to take the grandkids?

Where can you find the best options for a last-minute getaway? How can you feel confident you're getting a bargain? Let's take a look at some specific aspects of travel. It can be an exciting and rewarding way to spend some of those 168 hours per week as you reprogram your time in the second half of your life.

WHERE TO START

Travel is often at the top of the list of activities that retirees say they look forward to during the less stressful years after their primary career is "history." One of the big decisions people who are not seasoned travelers face is whether to travel with a group or to plan the trip yourself and travel alone or with a small group of friends.

Visiting Italy on a two-week group trip planned by a large travel agency, for example, will not be the same trip that four friends might plan with a map and a rental car. With an agency, most of every day will be planned: transportation, sightseeing, meals, lodging, and for the most part, the cost is up front. You might also have the opportunity to make some new friends. If you make your own plans, you have the opportunity to change those plans on a whim and explore new places you stumble across.

What kind of traveler are you? Do you want a knowledgeable guide to lead you through unknown places and help you understand the new culture or are you more likely to strike out on your own, meet the local people, and create your own itinerary?

Frequent travelers Lesley and Fred K. share a few thoughts and tips on do-it-yourself travel.

Fred and I discovered a love for travel when we were still just dating and our college team went to the Rose Bowl. We traveled with friends on the charter trip to California, and instead of just lounging by the pool during the days leading up to the game, we bought a guidebook and rented a car. Over the years we enjoyed many family vacations with our four children, but once the youngest was in junior high we realized our dream of taking a "just us" vacation and traveled to Europe. Since then we have gone to Europe at least 20 times and have planned each trip ourselves. Sometimes the vacations are months in planning, and others are much more spontaneous. A new destination requires more preparation, but stumbling across a great airfare to London may inspire us to book tickets for the next weekend! Here are some things that work well for us.

1. If you're traveling to a new country and you'll be visiting several cities, try going to a smaller city first. For example, arriving in Paris after an overnight flight can be overwhelming and even discouraging. Try taking a train or driving to the Normandy coast or the Barbizon Forest area and settling in for a few days. You'll be much more comfortable with the language, the pace, and the culture and ready to get the most out of your time in Paris.

2. Do your homework. We usually read multiple guidebooks to get a good overview. After our basic plan is in place, we select hotels for at least the first and last destinations. Many hotels can be booked online, or you can call the hotel directly. Don't hesitate to ask for special offers. We once traveled to London at the last minute and called our favorite hotel,

and I discovered that dinner and two tickets to a play of our choice was included if we stayed three nights. We prefer smaller independent hotels, inns, or guesthouses instead of chain hotels. Often, the hotel owner was the person to welcome us and ask us to sign the guest register. Experiences like this often set the tone for our overall European experience. Karen Brown's books are an excellent reference for charming places to stay, and they offer good sample itineraries.

3. We have found Rick Steves's books to be our favorite resources in planning what to see and do. Trip after trip, his recommendations have been right on target.

4. Whenever possible, take guided walking tours. There is no better way to really understand and appreciate what you are seeing. We usually feel very smart and informed after going on a walking tour, and the guides are excellent resources for restaurant recommendations.

5. If we miss a sight, or wish we had more time to spend in a particular locale, we always promise ourselves we will come back . . . and we do. The second time around (or third or fourth!), we are much more confident in our choices and find the return trips especially enjoyable.

6. Our experience has shown that it is easier and cheaper to reserve our rental car before we leave the states. Also, rates can be significantly less for a car with standard transmission.

7. Forget about traveler's checks; cash machines are everywhere. Don't spend a lot of time figuring out how to save pennies here or there in exchanging money.

Be brave, plan your own trip if you wish, and enjoy learning about the culture when you spend time with the locals. Remember, spending the first few days in a small town will make you more comfortable in the big city. Don't be afraid to return to the same location. As they say, the third time's the charm!

Linda and Frank B. take the attitude of "leave the planning to them" (the tour groups) when traveling to a foreign locale.

When we plan trips to any remote or exotic location such as Africa, China, Machu Pichu, or the Galápagos Islands, we choose to go by guided tour. Safety and health are our primary concerns, but language barriers, difficult climates, political changes, and cultural differences also present challenges for most travelers that are best dealt with by competent tour companies. For example, while in Kenya, a member of our group was hurt in an accident while we were tenting on the Masai Mara. Our group leader contacted Nairobi, had a plane dispatched to our grass landing strip to collect the injured woman and her spouse, flew them back to the city, and had a representative meet them plane-side and whisk them to a private hospital where she received excellent care (her MRI cost was $12.00!). She was then taken by the representative (who waited with the spouse at the hospital) to a hotel and checked into their room. The same representative returned the next morning to escort them to the doctor's office for a checkup and then returned them to the hotel. All this was part of the tour's service for its clients. I cannot imagine doing all that on one's own while trying to speak and understand Swahili!

When most of us think of taking guided tours, the image of the old movie, *If It's Tuesday, This Must Be Belgium,* pops into our heads. However, the idea of spending an entire trip on a bus, trying to cover as much ground as possible in a ten-day period, is not the type of tour we're discussing. The groups we travel with are limited in size and focus on an in-depth immersion so that at the end of the trip, we will not only have seen fabulous sights, but with the help of our guides, we will have an understanding of the importance of the places we have visited as well as the history and culture of the people who live there. Using our trip to Africa as an example once again, we had one guide who traveled with us day and night. Drivers and guides in each country we visited supported her. All were well-versed in history and anthropology, and the drivers were fully trained mechanics (a good idea when driving in the bush!

Did you know that "safari" literally means driving in circles?), which, combined, gave us a wonderful education while allowing us to be totally at ease in our surroundings.

From our point of view, one of the best things about traveling with a group is the people we meet. Though we all arrive at our destination as strangers, we already have several things in common, such as an interest in that particular part of the world, a sense of adventure, and a love of travel. We have met fascinating people from all over the world and have become life-long friends with some. On the other side of the coin, it is a given that in every group there will be someone who is perpetually late, or complains about the food, or should have simply stayed home. However, the guides are trained to contain the negativity, and, overall, it is a minor hiccup!

Finally, if you are thinking of taking an exotic trip, research tour groups that specialize in the part of the world you wish to experience. There are many excellent companies to choose from, such as Lindblad if you have a hankering for taking an ice breaker to the North Pole (they have their own ships and oceanographers), or Abercrombie and Kent if you're heading to Africa (they have been there for decades and own their own jeeps, which is important because they control the maintenance of the vehicles, train their drivers and guides, and are well connected with the various governments). Pesky details such as check-ins at airports and hotels are done behind the scenes, luggage is handled for you, and your guides truly educate you and want you to have a great experience. It's a win-win way to travel!

Okay, let's think about your destination. If you have the desire to travel, are not in the mood for a repeat trip to your favorite spot, and are feeling adventurous, these Web sites will be the encouragement you need to branch out and take a leap.

www.about.com/travel will make you feel more confident in choosing a novel location. Here you'll find information about what visitors need to know when traveling in Europe, the United States, or Asia. Find out about the latest budget-travel tips, the best B and Bs, or maybe the latest scuba diving information.

www.ricksteves.com/tours has been conducting all-inclusive budget tours since the 1970s. Rick Steves also publishes a series of guidebooks that concentrate on Europe, and he has had a travel show on PBS since 1991.

www.officialtravelinfo.com helps with destination information, vacation planning, and tourism information and provides virtual tours. Click on a map to choose your desired location. It can be fun to take a virtual tour in Africa, even if you have no plans to travel there.

www.go-today.com offers city and country packages, cruises, and unique tours at budget prices.

www.towd.com As the Web site states, "The Tourism Offices Worldwide Directory is your guide to official tourist information sources: government tourism offices, convention and visitors bureaus, chambers of commerce, and similar organizations that provide free, accurate, and unbiased travel information to the public. Businesses such as travel agents, tour operators, and hotels are not included."

www.atlasnavigator.com links to virtually every airline, airport, hotel chain, and car-rental agency in the world. Everything is in one location! Check out all travel options at once.

www.infohub.com lists guided or self-guided vacation options. Some categories to consider include: trips geared to active or soft adventure, families, hobbies, romance, spirituality, culture and history, sports, and nature and wildlife. You can also read travel stories and learn about these trips and the guides who lead them. How about taking a gourmet vacation and visiting various cooking schools?

www.shawguides.com *Forbes* and the *Wall Street Journal* pick this as a top site to give you literally thousands of choices for learning and creative career programs worldwide. Here are just a few: cultural travel, cooking schools, golf and tennis schools, photography workshops, language vacations, and writers' conferences and workshops.

According to the Travel Industry Association of America, adults 55 and over account for one-third of all trips taken within the United States.

---

www.resortquest.com has more than 20,000 vacation rental condominiums, villas, and homes in 16 states as well as in Canada.

www.tntvacations.com, **www.funjet.com**, and **www. vacationexpress.com** allow you to peruse different packages, then either book online or through a travel agent.

DISCOUNT TRAVEL

Chances are, the person sitting next to you on the airplane did not pay the same price for his or her ticket that you did. Two staterooms on a cruise liner boasting the same amenities can also have very different price tags.

What kind of shopper are you? Are you a full-price purchaser, ready to buy what you want when you want it? Are you willing to put up with the hassle of bargain shopping? Does price matter to you? If it does, and you look at getting a good deal as a challenge, keep reading and you'll find no end to the bargains available for travel. These budget tips work especially well for retirees, since many are last-minute opportunities, and retirees tend to be more spontaneous because time is not the ruling factor in their lives.

The best tool to use in bargain shopping for travel is the Internet; it will become your best travel agent. When choosing a Web site, find one that is easy for you to navigate since the market is flooded with sites, and you have many from which to choose. Check multiple sites carefully before trusting that one's rates are indeed the lowest. Use your own experiences from past travel as a comparison, and make a few phone calls directly to a hotel or airline, the old-fashioned way, just to be sure. Some Web sites post comments from fellow travelers revealing the positive and the negative aspects of their budget-travel experience. One way to look at bargain shopping for travel is that your savings can fund your next trip! So if words like discount, budget, bargain, good deal, and cut-rate are music to your ears, let your fingers do the walking through the Internet, and start packing!

WHERE TO STAY

Where to rest your weary head? Many budget options exist, including renting a villa, condo, or home for short-term or lengthy stays, or finding the ideal bed and breakfast or hotel. There are some outstanding places to stay that do not fit into the usual categories. Many active-adult communities offer inexpensive packages for a two-to four-day visit in exchange for a few hours of your time, universities offer rooms at reasonable prices in vibrant locations during their summer sessions, and even four- or five-star hotels offer lower prices if you know when to go. As with any agreement you enter into, however, *caveat emptor* (let the buyer beware). There can be restrictions, fees, penalties, etc., when booking travel, so read everything carefully!

www.globalfreeloaders.com is a free service that has more than 6,000 people in 100 countries willing to let you stay at their homes for free. (You need to be willing to do the same.)

www.evergreenclub.com (815-456-3111) is the "champion of the cost-conscious vacationer," according to Frommer's Budget Travel magazine. Joining the Evergreen Club ($30 for one person, $37.50 for two), allows people over 50 to access private homes and stay for rates of $15 per day for two people. Hosts provide clean, comfortable accommodations, hearty breakfasts, and acquaint you with their area.

www.lasvegas.com (866-678-2582) is a guide to bargains in Las Vegas (including shows, tours, and golf), as well as an opportunity to browse all the available hotels using a rating system that allows you to compare amenities and prices.

www.vacationrentals.com is a service for rental owners and renters. If you wish to rent, just click on the desired vacation location (both U.S. and international) and contact the property owner directly. You may also list, for free, a property you would like to rent.

www.ase.net searches more than 150,000 accommodations throughout the world and permits you to select the type of lodging, amenities, and price range you desire. This search engine can also show the results in different languages and display prices in various currencies.

www.hotels.com (800-246-8357 in the United States and Canada) claims to "have the best prices at the best places. Guaranteed." With more than 70,000 properties worldwide, this Web site has an extensive list of offerings.

www.quikbook.com (800-789-9887) has received kudos from *Condé Nast Traveler* magazine, *Forbes*

"Best of the Web," and Frommers.com. Quikbook promises no ads or pop-ups, just great values on upscale hotels without charging for cancellations or changes to your reservation. Choose from premier collections, seaside favorites, hip hotels, historic hotels, spa retreats, and many more.

www.bbonline.com (800-215-7365) allows you to choose from 5,200 bed and breakfasts in the United States, Canada, Mexico, and the Caribbean with the help of 20,000 color pictures.

www.innsite.com provides information, by location or activity, on bed and breakfasts, country inns, and small luxury hotels in more than 50 countries.

www.hiayh.org proves that hostels aren't just for young people! This Web site will lead you to affordable accommodations in more than 4,000 locations in 60 countries.

TIMESHARES/FRACTIONAL OWNERSHIP/INTERVAL OWNERSHIP

You can create a mini-vacation by signing up for a promotional stay offered by the timeshare/fractional ownership/interval ownership industry. Even if you have no intention of buying, you can enjoy these resort areas and learn what they have to offer. If you spend a few hours listening to their pitch (warning: they can be high-pressure), you can take advantage of a short stay in a nice area at a greatly reduced price. Or check to see if a timeshare resort is close to where you are planning to vacation and stay a few extra days, or perhaps receive a gift certificate to an area restaurant for your time. Only about ten percent of the visitors are persuaded to purchase a timeshare, but Cay S. visited one for fun and now is the happy owner of a week's stay in Duck, North Carolina. Look into offers from the Marriott Vacation Club International (www.vacationclub.com or 800-845-4226), the Hyatt Vacation Club (www.hyatt.com), or the Ritz-Carlton Club (www.ritzcarltonclub.com or 800-221-5780).

How about staying in a monastery? Just off the Chicago Loop, the Benedictines are rolling out the red carpet for $145 a night, www.chicagomonk.org, or if you are visiting Rome, check out www.santasusanna.org for recommendations in the Eternal City and other cities in Italy.

LAST-MINUTE DEALS

These Web sites are great for the spontaneous traveler who is looking for adventure and is ready to go at the drop of a hat. These opportunities can come and go very quickly, so if you see something perfect, grab it, but keep in mind that you probably won't be able to make changes or cancel your trip after you book it.

- www.site59.com (one-stop, real-time, last-minute [59th minute] weekend packages)
- www.11thhourvacations.com (cruises, flights, hotels, and vacation packages)
- www.lastminutetravel.com (cruises, cars, hotels, and flights)
- www.moments-notice.com (cars, cruises, hotels, and flights)
- www.hotwire.com (more last-minute deals)

HOME/HOSPITALITY EXCHANGE

Want to live like the locals? Stay in a neighborhood, shop where they shop, maybe drive their cars, almost literally walk a mile in their shoes? If this type of travel appeals to you, consider a home exchange or hospitality exchange. Home exchanges allow you to use someone else's home while they are using yours. Or, you could go the route of a hospitality exchange. In this type of arrangement, you alternate hosting one another in your homes. If you're considering a particular location for retirement, a home exchange might be the perfect way to "try out" a place.

There are obvious financial benefits to home or hospitality exchanges. The cost of hotel rooms is inching upward, and depending on the size of your group, you may need more than one hotel room. With a home exchange you have access to a full kitchen and all the comforts of home (or apartment, yacht, condo, RV, etc.). In addition, you can be immersed in the area and live where "real" people live. If you go the hospitality-exchange route, you'll also have built-in tour guides for your visit and may end up making lifelong friends.

The downside? Well, of course, it's all a matter of trust. Several months prior to your trip, it's a good idea to engage in conversations via e-mail, phone, or letters to get a sense of your swappers and the particulars about the residence. Also, there could be a question of parity. Switching a 1,000-square-foot apartment in Washington, DC, for a veritable chateau in France may not seem equal, but this should not be the point in home exchanges. Housekeeping standards can be an issue as well if your cleanliness habits differ appreciably. The abilities to be flexible in your scheduling, to compromise, and to plan in advance are important qualities for this type of travel.

When choosing a company to list or search properties, there are several things worth noting. When listing your home, provide a photo and be honest about its amenities. If you are exchanging cars, it's probably a good idea to get a contract. (Global Home Exchange offers a sample on their Web site—www.4homex.com.) Obtain insurance in case the trip is cancelled by either party. Make room in your closets for your visitors. Secure or remove any items you don't want used. Inform your neighbors there will be visitors so they can welcome them (and not call the police!). Come to a prior agreement on such things as phone and electric bills. Leave a guide containing information about your home's appliances, your area's attractions, contacts for repairs, etc. In general, being up-front and taking time to plan go a long way.

CRUISIN' THE USA

Since 9/11, more people have elected to vacation closer to home, traveling to places they can drive to themselves. So, although piling the kids in the van or station wagon every summer may be a thing of the past for you, this mode of travel is now at an all-time high.

And it's not just travel by car. Purchases of motorcycles and recreation vehicles have increased, notably among baby boomers. People who have never bought a motorcycle in their lives are now "easy riders." About 33 percent of Harley customers are first-time purchasers, and the surge in buyers over 40 has increased the average age of new Harley owners to 45 years old. Recreational-vehicle acquisition has also seen a significant increase. In a 2006 survey conducted by the National Association of RV Parks and Campgrounds (ARVC), the demographic profile of an RV owner in the United States comes as no surprise. Almost 9 million adults own RVs, with the greatest number being boomers. Grandparents make up about 63 percent of all RV owners!

If you go the route of driving yourself when you travel, there are several options to ease your journey on the long and winding road. Almost everyone is familiar with the American Automobile Association (AAA). This organization has been in existence for more than a century. Perks of membership include road service, maps, towing, TripTiks (which can be printed from your computer), tour books, books listing RV sites and campgrounds, recommended driving trips, insurance, discounts, and other services. Membership fees are approximately $58 annually but can vary if you add additional members of the family to your plan or wish to extend your coverage options. With various AAA discounts, the membership fee can more than pay for itself.

There are also several clubs specifically for RVers, such as the Good Sam Club (www.goodsams. net), Coast to Coast (access through www.rv.net or 800-368-5721), and Escapees RV Club (www.escapees. com). If you're single, that doesn't mean you have to go it alone. Several clubs include Loners on Wheels (www.lonersonwheels.com), Retired Singles (www.retiredsingles.com), and RVing Women (www. rvingwomen.org or 888-557-8464), which, as the name implies, is for females who either own a RVs or would like to become part of the RV lifestyle.

You can also become part of a pack if you choose to travel by cycle. The American Motorcyclist Association (www.amadirectlink.com) was founded in 1924 and has more than 260,000 members. It provides services similar to those of AAA. Great American Motorcycle Touring (www.greatamericantouring. com or 800-727-3390) offers tours, self-guided tours, and custom tours. No bike? No problem! You can rent one through GAMT if you don't own one or don't wish to ship or drive yours to the departure city. Retreads Motorcycle Club International (www.retreads.org) has two requirements to join: a love of biking and an age of at least 40.

SOLO TRAVEL

The single traveler is anything but alone! The Travel Industry Association notes that this segment of the travel business accounted for about 30 percent of all U.S. travel in 2004; a staggering 38 million middle-aged singles (average age 45) took a solo trip. Although some of these were business trips, leisure travel accounted for almost 70 percent. The increase in the number of single people, coupled with the affluence of these age groups, has contributed to this fast-growing trend.

Many people feel comfortable traveling alone, responsible only for themselves in choosing an itinerary, selecting restaurants, arranging their schedule, etc. The once-upon-a-time perceived stigma of a woman traveling alone has largely disappeared, although common sense should be exercised whether you are male or female.

If you're contemplating traveling solo, but are a little uncomfortable with the concept, travel guru Arthur Frommer recommends considering volunteer or learning vacations. A trip that has an outer-directed goal with like-minded participants often works well. Earthwatch, the Sierra Club, Elderhostel, the Omega Institute, and Habitat for Humanity all sponsor these types of trips. For more specifics on this kind of travel, see the section on "Volunteer Vacations" on page 71 and the suggested reading.

If you're looking for trips that cater to mature singles, several companies fit the bill. Windjammer Barefoot Cruises (www.windjammerbarefoot.com) has sailings designated specifically for singles. Celebrity, Cunard, Crystal, Seabourn, Silversea, Radisson, and Holland America are other cruise lines to investigate and often provide gentleman hosts for dancing and dining. Of course, if you're a man looking to socialize, choosing one of these cruise lines would be good planning as well. Adventure travel also attracts large numbers of mature singles—try Overseas Adventure Travel (www.oattravel.com or 800-493-6824) or Back-roads (www.backroads.com or 800-462-2848).

If you are happy traveling alone but don't want to underwrite the cost of a room or cabin by yourself, you also have several options. Often, the cruise line or company (such as Club Med) will arrange a roommate to avoid the single-supplement charge for singles staying in a double room. Occasionally, single-supplement charges will be waived; it never hurts to ask! Several organizations will set you up with a roommate as well. O Solo Mio (www.osolomio.com or 800-959-8568) has been around for more than ten years and arranges singles' tours both nationally and internationally.

O Solo Mio will match you with a same-sex person of similar age, smoking preferences, and sleeping habits (i.e., night owl or early bird). All Singles Travel (www.allsinglestravel.com or 800-717-3231) will also match you with a roommate to avoid the single supplement.

Got kids? Single Parent Tours (www.singleparenttours.com or 877-464-6778) is a great place to look for a trip for a single parent and the children!

More daring is the free classified-ad service you can access through Aim-Higher Travel (www.aim-higher.com or 877-752-1858). This organization has been in business since 1998 and also deals in singles' cruises and tours. Another possibility for finding traveling companions includes the free message board on www.travelchums.com, where you can fill out a questionnaire online.

If you're female, there are travel groups designed specifically for you, such as Gutsy Women Travel (www.gutsywomentravel.com or 866-464-8879).

A little off the beaten path is Sacred Sites Tours (www.sacredsitestours.com or 612-823-2442). This group leads small groups (12 or fewer) of women and girls on tours of mythical, historical, and other enchanted spots in England and Scotland.

How about Shop Around Tours (www.shoparoundtours.com or 212-684-3763)? Go in search of a good deal on an insider's bargain-hunting trip to Italy.

Women Welcome Women World Wide (5W) at www.womenwelcomewomen.org.uk is an international-travel group that enables women of different countries to visit one another and helps to foster friendship, connections, and cross-cultural under-standing. This company has been around for more than 20 years and currently has 3,000 members in 70 countries. There is a membership fee.

Here's a tip: If you drop your camera in water, let it sit overnight in a bag of rice. The rice will draw out the condensation. (Source: *Budget Travel*)

GROUP TRAVEL

More than a quarter of the U.S. population is over 50, and by 2020 this number is expected to increase by one-third. This may be news to you, but it's not news to tour companies! Travel companies are cropping up to cater exclusively to the mature traveler (50 to 55 and older), and companies that have been in existence for many years recognize the power of the baby-boomer market. Senior travelers are more often than not interested in the ease and comfort that a tour affords. Travel companies that court seniors offer soft adventure, luxury cruises, educational opportunities, and tours that combine all three.

Making the decision to travel with a group instead of traveling on your own seems to be a path many boomers are taking. Tour companies eliminate the planning details, and for the budget conscious, tours are often the better bargain. When airfares, hotels, and food are purchased in great quantities, the price goes down (of course, you do sacrifice spontaneity). Tours that are designed for the mature traveler give more attention to health and mobility issues, with slower-paced days and comfortable nights. Some even promise that you won't need to have your suitcase ready by 6 a.m. every day!

A good place to start looking if you are interested in booking a tour would be the companies that have been in existence for many years. These companies specialize in tours that vary greatly in cost, from budget to luxury. Most travel companies will customize a tour for you if you provide your own group consisting of 15 people or more. Dozens of good companies exist.

Grand Circle Tours (www.gct.com or 800-959-0405). In existence since 1958, GCT agrees with John Steinbeck that "people don't take trips, trips take people." Prices vary greatly, as do the locations.

Globus and Cosmos Tours (www.globusandcosmos.com.) The Globus family offers great group travel.

Tauck Tours (www.tauck.com or 800-788-7885). A family business since 1925, and more than half of its travelers repeat customers, Tauck has won more than 50 awards and is known for its all-inclusive, upscale travel.

Trafalgar Tours (www.trafalgar-tours.net) has been in existence for around 60 years. Take escorted motor-coach tours to a variety of destinations worldwide. One of the authors accompanied her elderly mother, along with two sisters, on a nine-day Trafalgar tour of Italy. Although some excursions were extra, and the hotels were mediocre, prices were reasonable, and they enjoyed the services of a terrific tour guide.

"SOFT" ADVENTURE TRAVEL

If the same old trip to the beach doesn't sound like enough this year, give some thought to learning new skills and trying them out in a fresh place. Many mature travelers are ready and willing to try a new venture, especially with a group of their peers and the promise of creature comforts at the end of the day. There is no end to the opportunities if you are ready to take the plunge. An adventure cruise with

Elderhostel will take you sailing on the Dingle Peninsula of Ireland, or maybe you would like to explore the Galápagos Islands. Perhaps you'd like to start out easy and ride a bike from Cumberland, Maryland, to the nation's capital and stay at upscale bed and breakfasts along the way. Whatever you choose to do, and wherever you choose to take your adventure, there is a trip for you.

Abercrombie & Kent. This tour company has been in business for 45 years and offers upscale adventure tours on all seven continents. Expect the very best in accommodations. Contact www.abercrombiekent.com or 800-554-7016.

Country Walkers. Explore new environs on foot with an experienced guide, choosing from a number of worldwide tours. Stroll through a village in Greece or kayak down a river in New Zealand. Country Walkers has more than 25 years of experience, and they promise to deliver an exhilarating adventure. Contact www. countrywalkers.com or 800-464-9255.

New England Hiking Holidays. "Footpaths by day! And Country inns by night!" Enjoy the expertise of more than two decades of successful trips and the comfort of knowing that two guides accompany each trip—one for the fast walkers and one for the slightly slower group! Take a walking trip within the United States, Canada, or Europe, or sign up for a multiadventure, which combines walking with kayaking, snorkeling, or biking. Contact www.nehikingholidays. com or 800-869-0949.

Elder Treks. With a 20-year history, Elder Treks offer adventures in 80 countries for the 50-plus age group. Plow your way through the ice pack to the North Pole on an icebreaker, or explore Mongolia by camel. Contact www.eldertreks.com or 800-741-7956.

Senior Cycling. No one is concerned with how far or how fast you go; you can choose your own level of difficulty. These "old folks on spokes" offer bicycle trips throughout the United States. Contact www.seniorcycling.com or 540-668-6307.

Walking the World. Experience the world as an active participant. "You'll get to know an area not by how it looks through the window of a bus, but by its true flavor!" Since 1978, Walking the World's trips "for people 50 and better" include such places as Costa Rica, Switzerland, Italy, and Germany. Contact www.walkingtheworld.com or 877-340-9255.

Elderhostel. With thousands of participants enjoying thousands of varied trips in many different countries, choosing an adventure will be your greatest problem! Contact www.elderhostel.org or 800-454-5768

Travel Quest International. Things are looking up! Travel Quest International offers astronomy-related tours to such places as China, Costa Rica, Russia, and on the seas (through Princess Cruise Lines). Contact www.tq-international.com or 800-830-1998.

Travel Without Temptation. Sober Travel Adventures (www.sobertraveladventures.com or 770-432-8225), Meetings en Route (www.sober-sailors.org or 866-678-8785), or Sober Vacations

International (www.sobervacations.com or 800-762-3738). Enjoy meetings and speakers as well as snorkeling, scuba, golf, and other great holiday activities. "Alcohol-free vacations for people who crave adventure . . . one day at a time!"

World Wildlife Fund. Travel the world and see spectacular wildlife in its natural habitat. WWF trips are geared for young adults through active seniors. Contact www.worldwildlife.org/travel or 888-993-8687.

50plus Expeditions. Exotic travel for the 50-and-up group. Trips are rated easy, moderate, or demanding, and locations include the Arctic, Antarctica, Asia, East Africa, Latin America, and North America. Contact www.50plusexpeditions.com or 866-318-5050.

Adventure Network International. This group specializes in Antarctica. You can choose a trip from luxury level to extreme-endurance level. Prepare to bundle up! Contact www.adventure-network.com or 801-266-4876.

Most automobile rental agencies start their weekend rates at noon on Thursday and end at midnight on Sunday. You can often obtain better rates during this time frame.

LEARNING VACATIONS

Budget traveler Gary Langer once wrote, "Travelers and tourists, the distinction is simple: Tourists are those who bring their homes with them wherever they go, and apply them to whatever they see. They are closed to experiences outside of the superficial. Travelers, however, leave home at home, bringing only themselves and a desire to learn." If you feel as Mr. Langer does and want more out of your next vacation, you may be ready for a learning vacation, or the most fabulous field trip you have ever taken! Check out the following.

www.closeup.org/lifelong.htm   (800-256-7387). Would you like to spend a week in our nation's capital and learn what makes it work? In cooperation with Elderhostel, the Close Up Foundation offers a week-long program combining a vacation with firsthand knowledge of our nation's capital.

www.travelearn.com   (800-235-9114). With 25 years of experience, TraveLearn provides learning vacations for "people who take their minds with them on vacation." As an example, you can experience the archaeology, ecology, and culture of Peru during a 16-day excursion that includes lectures and seminars.

www.smithsonianjourneys.org   (877-338-8687). Smithsonian Journeys has been a leader in educational travel for more than three decades. Thousands of travelers have enjoyed the network of resources available to the Smithsonian that make this a unique travel and learning experience. The itineraries range from a guided tour of the Metropolitan Opera to 17 days in Burma.

www.unex.berkeley.edu/travel (510-642-3824).
London theater, China's ancient cities, Sicilian mosaics! "We invite you to take more than just a trip. Please join us for a challenging intellectual adventure." The average age of participants is 50 to 60 years old in this "Travel with Scholars" extension of UC-Berkeley. Two years of college is a prerequisite for the Oxford program.

www.amnh.org—click on "AMNH Expeditions" (800-462-8687). The American Museum of Natural History has been offering educational travel for more than 50 years. More than 20,000 travelers have explored the world on AMNH Expeditions—from pole to pole and everywhere in between—in the company of AMNH scientists.

www.metmuseum.org (212-650-2110). Click on "Events and Programs," then "Travel Programs." And what programs they have! You will enjoy reading about these trips even if you never go; check out "Temples, Gods, and Gardens: The Greek Isles."

www.elderhostel.org Elderhostel and Specialty Travel also offers a wide variety of educational travel, including biblical tours, cooking tours, and tours that focus on birding, antiquing, creative workshops, and adventures afloat. Plan to spend some time on these Web sites; the opportunities are endless.

www.princess.com (800-774-6237). The educational program on Princess Cruise Lines is cleverly titled ScholarShip@Sea. Classes in computer technology, culinary/creative/visual arts, and other special topics (such as spelling bees!) are offered.

www.soulplanettravel.com and **www.soulo-famerica.com** are two travel organizations responding to the needs and desires of African-Americans to patronize African-American-owned bed and breakfasts and hotels and to participate in African-American culture tours, cruises, etc.

VOLUNTEER VACATIONS

Vacation: "A time of respite; a scheduled period during which activity is suspended; a period of exemption from work granted to an employee for rest and relaxation." If Merriam-Webster's definition of "vacation" is accurate, then what does volunteering have to do with vacationing? Most people look upon public service as a punishment issued by a judge in lieu of jail time. It may be difficult to believe, but tens of thousands of people the world over are scheduling time away to be of service to others. The idea is to help yourself while helping others. If retirement seems to be lacking in purpose and fulfillment, take a look at the voluntourism opportunities that might provide adventure for you and help for those who really need it.

Cross-Cultural Solutions (www.crosscultural-solutions.org or 800-380-4777) is a not-for-profit international volunteer organization that operates in Africa, Asia, Eastern Europe, and Latin America. The New York Times refers to Cross-Cultural Solutions as "akin to a mini-stint with the Peace Corps." Work may include caring for infants, teaching teenagers, helping set up a small business for working adults, as well as providing the local people the opportunity to learn about your culture.

Farm Sanctuary (www.farmsanctuary.org or 607-583-2225) in New York cares for injured, abused, or abandoned farm animals and promotes a vegan lifestyle. You can help out with farm chores or office work. If your interest leans more toward pets than farm animals, contact Best Friends Animal Sanctuary (www.bestfriends.org or 435-644-2001). This is the largest pet sanctuary in the United States, is located near Kanab, Utah, and cares for an astounding 1,500 cats, dogs, and other pets.

Global Volunteers (www.globalvolunteers.org or 800-487-1074) offers more than 150 one-, two-, or three-week projects year-round. Volunteers are involved in painting and constructing homes, tutoring school-children, improving public health, and teaching English. Global Volunteers are at work in more than "100 host communities in 20 countries on six continents."

The Flying Doctors (www.flyingdocs.org or 800-585-4568) enables volunteers to provide nonskilled assistance in setting up a clinic and providing medical and dental services in Mexico, Central America, and the Coachella Valley of California in the United States.

Habitat for Humanity (www.habitat.org or 800-422-4828) volunteers work in foreign countries as well as throughout the United States. "Habitat has built more than 200,000 houses around the world, providing more than 1,000,000 people in more than 3,000 communities with safe, decent, affordable shelter." The opportunities are extensive.

If you have an RV or have always wanted to rent one, try **RV Care-A-Vanners.** This group works with Habitat affiliates. A Care-A-Van usually lasts two weeks and includes eight to 20 volunteers. Participants travel together and work together at the Habitat sites. Bring tools, energy, enthusiasm, and flexibility! You can contact RV Care-A-Vanners at rvinfodesk@habitat.org.

Earthwatch Institute (www.earthwatch.org or 800-776-0188) is involved in ongoing research run by members of the scientific community. In 2006, Earthwatch sponsored more than 155 research projects in 48 countries and 16 U.S. states. Topics include ecology, zoology, archaeology, world health, and more. Earthwatch provides short-term volunteer opportunities lasting about ten to 14 days. Some weekend opportunities exist.

American Hiking Society (www.americanhiking. org or 301-565-6704) provides a rewarding experience while visiting picturesque backcountry locations. Meet new people while constructing footpaths or rebuilding existing trails, cabins, and shelters. Enjoy evenings around the campfire and rest up for another great day outdoors. Similar Web sites to check are www.wildernessvolunteers.org and www.sierraclub. org (click on "get outdoors").

In general, when researching volunteer vacations, you'll need to find out the specifics from the organization in which you're interested, such as age requirements, your expenses (which can vary tremendously depending on the trip), time frames, any special abilities or physical level required, what to wear, what to bring, and how you apply to the program. As far as tax deductions go, you will need to find out what's eligible from the IRS and your tax advisor. At a minimum, the organization must be nonprofit and tax exempt, which many of these organizations are. Items that may be deductible (assuming you itemize on your tax return) include auto mileage, tolls, parking, food, and lodging. Of course, this applies only if the purpose of the travel is volunteering. Keep careful records! You can call the IRS for help at 800-829-1040; if hearing-impaired, call 800-829-4059.

A volunteer vacation is not an oxymoron. There are hundreds of volunteer organizations around the world just waiting to hear from you.

In most cases, your driver's license is all that is necessary to rent or drive a vehicle in another country, but some countries require an international driver's license or special insurance. Contact an organization such as AAA or a rental agency in the country you are planning to visit for details.

TRAVELING WITH GRANDCHILDREN

Traveling with your grandchildren can deepen relationships and create lifelong memories. This type of travel ranks high on the trips mature travelers would like to take. In fact, in a survey of group travelers by the National Tour Association and Group Leaders of America, travel involving grandparents and grandchildren ranked ninth out of the top 50 tours and destinations available.

The leader in grandparent/grandchild travel is Grandtravel (www.grandtrvl.com or 800-247-7651). This organization has been around for about 20 years. Grandtravel offers national and international itineraries designed to be enjoyed by both generations; teachers or leisure counselors escort the trips. Tours, scheduled primarily in the summer months, include Greece, Alaska, Kenya, Australia, and France.

The Sagamore Foundation (www.sagamore.org or 315-354-5311) offers a grandparent/grandchild summer camp in New York's Adirondack Mountains that includes hikes, indoor and outdoor activities, and campfires. Register through Elderhostel. Elderhostel also offers a large number of intergenerational trips of varying lengths and destinations (www.elderhostel. org or 800-454-5768).

TRUE LIFE: PHIL AND CAROL W. . . .

Phil and Carol W. are experienced travelers, authors of "Live Your Road Trip Dream," and most of all, grandparents who love to create travel memories with their ever-expanding tribe of grandchildren. At last count they lay claim to 11, ranging in age from six months to 17 years old, including some "steps" along the way.

Phil and Carol are young retirees who believe that creating memories with their grandchildren is much more important than what they give their grandchildren. "We could never compete with the outpouring of 'things' from the parents and other more distant grandparents, so we decided early on to make our presence known by being present with the kids as they grew," comments Phil. "It has really developed in us a sense of who each of them is as people, and they will surely look back on growing up, feeling that they really knew Grammie and Wookies," adds Carol. (Grandpa Phil used to have a beard and became known as "Whiskers" to the first grandchild. Later, another grandchild couldn't yet say "Whiskers" so it came out "Wookies," and the name has stuck ever since.)

The 48-Inch Trip

When the first two of the grandchildren reached the size to go on the big rides at Disneyland, we decided that would make a fun excursion for all of us. Who doesn't love Disneyland, especially with a wide-eyed eight and nine-year-old in tow?

In the years that have followed, each grandchild anxiously anticipates their turn for their "48-inch trip." The most recent two had already been to Disneyland many times, so it seemed a lot less special as the time drew near to plan the trip. We looked for alternatives, discussed choices with them, and decided on San Diego, California, instead. We all had a great adventure.

We take them two at a time (always cousins—much better than siblings from both an economic and companionship viewpoint) and find that it has worked well. Now that the Disneyland requirement has been broken, we're sure that each set of "48 inchers" will want to put their own marks on their special trips with us.

Lessons Along the Way

Kids are such great sponges. They absorb everything that they see and hear, especially when on their best behavior traveling with us. We take the time alone with them to really learn about them and to impart bits of wisdom that we learned over the years. We know they find some of what we say "quaint" (or worse!), but we also know that they do absorb life lessons from us too.

Each summer we team up with another set of grandparents and take all those who are ages five and above and who want to go on an outing. It started out as just a day trip, but each year gets more elaborate. One thing that has been consistent from the beginning has been the "teaching moments."

One year it was learning about the Lewis and Clark

expedition as we traveled via train to Fort Clatsop in Oregon, where the party stayed the winter. A large book with lots of pictures (borrowed from the library) formed the basis for talking about the adventure. Last year, we went to Wildlife Safari (a drive-through wild-animal park in Oregon). Before we left, each child was assigned an animal we would see in the park and had to do an oral report in front of the others. Such moaning you have never heard! They tried everything to get out of it. But once they all got into it over pizza at the motel, they really learned a lot. They asked questions of each other, the older ones helped the little ones, and it turned out to be an overall great experience that they still talk about. This year the trip was river rafting. We got creative and had each child decorate their own "River Rat Hat," which was then judged by the guides. Their creations definitely reflected their own personalities!

No matter what we do, we always try to find a way to expand their knowledge and have fun in the process. We think it is a formula that they will remember long after last year's toys are gone.

If planning a trip on your own, consider a cruise. The more family-oriented cruise lines include Disney, Carnival, Princess, Norwegian (especially the Norwegian Dawn), and Royal Caribbean. Destinations such as dude ranches (for example, the Triangle C Dude Ranch in Wyoming, www.trianglec.com, click on "Dude Ranch Vacations," or call 800-661-4928), resorts that cater to families, spas that allow adult indulgence yet provide activities for kids, and fascinating cities are other possibilities.

The financial costs of traveling with grandchildren can vary, but the emotional rewards can be priceless!

> "Travel and change of place impart new vigor to the mind."
> —Seneca

TRAVELING WITH PHYSICAL DISABILITIES

It's estimated that between 50 million and 65 million Americans have some type of disability. The travel industry is responding to this huge market. Don't let the fact that you need a scooter or wheelchair to get around slow you down. If you are hearing or vision impaired, need dialysis, require oxygen, or have other disabilities, you can still enjoy travel. You may need to do more homework than others, but accessible travel is out there.

Various travel organizations specialize in meeting access needs. Accessible Journeys (www.disability-travel.com or 800-846-4537) organizes group trips and cruises, helps with independent travel, and can provide a health-care professional as a travel companion. Nautilus Tours and Cruises (www.nautilustours.com or 818-591-3159) and Flying Wheels Travel (www.flyingwheelstravel.com or 507-451-5005) also assist with disabled travelers, both nationally and internationally. Access-Able Travel Source (www.access-able.com) disseminates information on travel agents, cruises, accommodations, equipment rental, etc. Wilderness Inquiry (www.wildernessinquiry.org or 800-728-0719) has been in business since 1978 and promotes inclusion of all ability levels and ages in the exploration of wild areas. One example is hiking and kayaking in Misty Fjords National Monument, Alaska.

If you have physical challenges, taking a cruise can be one of the better ways to vacation. New ships are being built with accessibility in mind, and older ships are being retrofitted to ensure smooth sailing with staterooms and hallways that accommodate wheelchairs and scooters; pools with lifts; newsletters, elevator buttons, and menus in Braille; amplified telephones; close-captioned TVs; roll-in showers; and lower closet bars and sinks. Ports of call and shore excursions are becoming more accessible as well. Contact the access desk at the appropriate cruise line to discuss your needs. Now you don't have to miss the boat!

On a broader note, resource organizations for the disabled include Mobility International USA (www.miusa.org or 541-343-1284) and the Society for Accessible Travel and Hospitality (SATH), which can be contacted at www.sath.org or 212-447-7284. One of the goals of Mobility International is to promote "the inclusion of disabled people in all types of exchange, community, and volunteer-service programs." SATH works to provide barrier-free travel both nationally and internationally, provides tips on travel (such as how to travel with a speech impairment), and provides a good resource list for the disabled traveler.

So now you're ready, willing, and able. Take the attitude of Pastor Charles Swindoll, who said, "The longer I live, the more convinced I become that life is ten percent what happens to us and 90 percent how we respond to it." Bon voyage!

The U.S. National Park Service offers a Golden Access Passport that gives free lifetime entrance to U.S. national parks for persons who are permanently disabled, regardless of age.

PART THREE

...

How do you enjoy
retirement for years to come?

BE FOREVER YOUNG

...

"You can get old pretty young
if you don't take care of yourself."
—Yogi Berra

Average life expectancy has increased from 49 years in 1901 to 78 years today. And if you are a 65-year-old female, odds are you'll live to 85. What will you do with this gift of 30 or more years?

How can you stay healthy—physically as well as emotionally? Most of us want to live a long, long life. A 2005 Pew Research Survey found that 43 percent of people surveyed want to reach the ripe old age of 100. Of course, we want these years to be better, not just longer. But how do we accomplish that? According to Dr. Walter Bortz, a scientific expert on aging, genes account for about one-fifth of our longevity, and our lifestyle choices account for four-fifths. As Dr. Bortz states, "Living longer is a choice, not fate. Living longer is active, not passive. You create your own destiny."

The trick, therefore, is to capitalize on those things we can control. How can we be proactive and stave off disease? Does looking better help us feel better? And what are the financial repercussions of living longer? With nursing homes costing an average of more than $75,000 a year, according to a 2006 MetLife Survey, and medical experts bemoaning the shortage of geri-atricians, it's in our best interest to remain as healthy as possible. Finally, since death is inevitable (along with taxes, of course!), how can we help our aging parents—and ourselves—prepare for this final act of our lives?

The phrase carpe diem translates to "seize the day" and includes the concept of "eat, drink, and be merry, for tomorrow we may die." So let's start with that thought. How should we eat, drink, and be merry?

As of 2007, the oldest documented living person is 114-year-old Yone Minagawa, a Japanese woman born in 1893.

"EAT, DRINK . . ."

From Atkins to the Zone, the way you choose to eat really does run the gamut from A to Z! Notice we didn't use the word diet. Strike that word from your vocabulary, since it conjures up images of deprivation, and it's often used as a short-term means to achieve a goal of losing weight, followed by a return to old habits. Instead, the idea is to foster a lifelong way of eating that is healthful and makes you feel good.

What is the best way to eat? Needless to say, judging from the millions of magazine articles, scientific studies, news reports, and books on the topic, nutrition is a field with many opinions and a lot of controversy. One reason is that, particularly in the area of losing weight, a certain approach may work for some people but not for others. There is, however, agreement in one area: Obesity is a huge and growing (no pun intended) problem in the United States. About 65 percent of adults are either overweight or obese, and obesity is associated with almost 30 medical conditions, including arthritis, some cancers, diabetes, coronary heart disease, and high blood pressure.

If we assess all the nutrition information that has been generated, several constants emerge.

Calories count. There is one ironclad rule that virtually no one disputes: To lose weight, the number of calories you burn has to exceed the number of calories you eat. To find out how many calories a certain food contains, go to www.caloriecontrol.org. This site also assesses your diet, offers recipes, and provides suggestions and tips for staying (or getting) healthy and fit.

High-quality carbohydrates are better for you. All carbs are not created equal. Think whole grains such as whole-wheat bread, whole-grain pasta, whole-grain cereals, oatmeal, fruits, and vegetables.

Highly processed grains should be avoided. These include white bread, white rice, white pasta, cake, doughnuts, pancakes, waffles, and sugary cereals that aren't whole grain.

Protein is a requirement of a healthy diet. How many grams of protein do you need every day? The answer depends on how active you are. If you're sedentary, you need about .4 grams of protein per pound of body weight. If you are strength-training on a regular basis, you'll need .8 grams of protein per pound of body weight in order to rebuild those muscle fibers you break down during your workout. Lean meats, fish, poultry, dairy products, legumes, and peanut butter are all good sources of protein. Keep in mind that foods that contain protein, water, and fiber have a higher fullness factor—you won't have to return to the fridge as frequently!

There are "good" fats and "bad" fats. Although the mantra has been to avoid all fats like the plague, more recent information has shown that, as with carbs, not all fats are created equal. Fats are necessary in the human body. There are two fatty acids our body can't manufacture: omega-6 (linoleic acid) and omega-3 (alpha-linoleic acid). We call these two "essential fatty acids" because they are essential to our health and life. In addition, fat in food adds flavor and gives us a feeling of satiety, or fullness.

The trick in eating fats is to choose those that are heart healthy, which means those that include monounsaturated and polyunsaturated (omega-6 and omega-3) fats; these are generally plant-based fats that tend to be liquid at room temperature. You will find them in canola, olive, and safflower oils, as well as fish (we know, not a plant) and nuts. In the United States, our ratio of omega-6 to omega-3 fats tends to be around 20:1; aim for a ratio between 3:1 and 5:1.

The fats to avoid are the saturated fats, which tend to be from land animals and are solid at room temperature (think lard, butter, and the fat streaks in red meat), and tropical oils (palm and coconut oil).

In addition to saturated fats and tropical oils, trans fats are another type of fat to avoid. Trans fats are found in margarine, baked goods, and fried foods. The FDA now requires trans fats to be listed separately on nutrition labels (unless the food is not a significant source of trans fat), which will make it easier to know how many grams of trans fat you're ingesting. Eat as few grams as possible.

Fiber is essential. The American Dietetic Association recommends that we ingest 20 to 35 grams of fiber every day, but most Americans get only about half that. Good sources of fiber include whole grain cereals; legumes such as kidney beans, black beans, and lentils; apples with the peels; and popcorn.

The glycemic index is an important tool. Some carbohydrates cause a rapid rise, then a rapid drop, in blood-sugar levels; these are called high-glycemic foods. Other carbohydrates cause a much slower, more even rise in blood-sugar levels; these are the low-glycemic foods. Studies done at Tufts University and elsewhere indicate that eating high-glycemic carbohydrates can lead to overeating, while other researchers have found evidence linking diabetes and heart disease with high-glycemic patterns of eating. Foods are classified as having a high glycemic index (70 or above), medium glycemic index (56 to 69), or low glycemic index (55 or less). For a list of the glycemic indexes of some common foods, go to http://www. mendosa.com/common_foods.htm or refer to *The New Glucose Revolution Shopper's Guide to GI Values* 2006 by Jennie Brand-Miller.

Water is good for you. Water is vital to health, and research presented at the Obesity Society's national convention in 2006 has shown it can also aid in weight loss. Researchers from the Oakland Research Institute in California found adult women who replaced sweetened drinks with water lost an average of 5 pounds more over a year's time than those who did not replace sugary drinks with water, and women who drank more than 4 cups of water a day lost 2 pounds more (over the course of a year) than those who did not drink as much as 4 cups a day.

Consume alcohol in moderation. There has been a lot of research on the relationship between alcohol consumption and heart disease, and studies demonstrate that moderate drinkers—women who have one drink a day and men who have one or two—have a lower risk of heart disease than nondrinkers. The American Heart Association does not recommend that you start drinking if you do not presently consume alcohol, however, since many more deaths, illnesses, accidents, and tragedies are associated with drinking than with not drinking.

> The American Institute for Cancer Research reports that from 30 to 40 percent of cancers could be prevented through better nutrition and other lifestyle choices.

EAT HEALTHY

Be proactive about your health, and help stave off disease, by keeping the aforementioned guidelines in mind. But knowing what you should eat is not enough; you need to know how much protein, fat, and carbohydrate you should consume each day. There are two ways to approach this problem: by understanding what percentage of your total intake each of these nutrients should represent and by using food pyramids, which graphically represent what you should eat.

The recommended percentages of various nutrients will differ depending on what diet you look at. Most, however, tend to emphasize nonprocessed foods, whole grains, and lean cuts of meat. The best-selling entry into the weight-loss melee, The South Beach Diet, restricts processed carbohydrates but is more liberal with the complex carbs than is Atkins.

If you go the percentage route, you will first need to know how many calories your body requires each day. There are several ways to calculate this. You can use an online calorie calculator such as www.inch-aweigh.com/dcn.php (click on "Calories Per Day" under "Weight-Loss Tools"), which takes into account gender, age, height, weight, and activity level, then calculates how many calories you need per day to maintain your present weight and how many calories you need if your goal is to lose weight. One pound is equal to 3,500 calories, so reducing your caloric intake (or increasing your activity level) to create a deficit of 500 calories a day will result in a loss of 1 pound per week. For healthy weight loss, don't attempt to lose any more than 1 or 2 pounds per week.

If math isn't your thing—or you have other things to do with your day than count calories—several food pyramids recommend the number of servings and kinds of food to eat. The Food Guide Pyramid is designed by the United States Department of Agriculture (USDA). The current version allows you to individualize your pyramid based on age, sex, and activity level. Go to www.mypyramid.gov to input your info.

Walter C. Willett, MD, of the Harvard School of Public Health, developed the Healthy Eating Pyramid, the foundation of which are physical activity and weight control. On the second level, whole grains are encouraged, and healthy unsaturated, monounsaturated, and polyunsaturated fats are given a prominent location on the Healthy Eating Pyramid. As far as fruits and veggies go, Dr. Willett excludes potatoes from the recommended vegetables, placing them at the top along with sweets and unrefined grains, which are to be eaten sparingly. Dr. Willett views nuts and legumes as healthier forms of protein, so he gives them their own level, and he places fish, poultry, and eggs (he suggests that red meats should be eaten less frequently) on a different level. He recommends fewer dairy products and suggests the use of a calcium supplement. Both pyramids reflect that sweets should be eaten frugally, but Dr. Willett also places foods that either have a high glycemic index or are high in saturated fat at the top of his pyramid. Moderate alcohol consumption is reflected in his pyramid, as is the taking of a daily multivitamin.

What's the moral of the story? You have to figure out what works for you. Keeping in mind the general guidelines discussed previously, healthy eating that keeps you at a good weight and feeling energetic is what works.

How often should you eat? Again, there is no one correct answer. Since it's not so much the frequency as the quality and quantity of what's ingested that counts, the number of meals that prevents you from overeating at the next chow time is the frequency that is right for you.

You know your chronological age, but what is your biological age? Take the free "RealAge Test" (go to www.realage.com and click on "RealAge Test"), which analyzes your lifestyle choices, and see how you can become younger!

TAKE YOUR VITAMINS

Finally, should you take supplements? Many of us do not get the DRI (dietary reference intake; this replaced the RDA—recommended dietary allowance—in 1997) of certain nutrients. As a result, most experts suggest or see no harm in taking a good multivitamin/mineral supplement every day.

One mineral that most Americans don't get enough of is calcium. The most abundant mineral in the body, calcium is responsible for healthy bones and teeth as well as nerve transmission and muscle contraction. Although most calcium is stored in the bones, if there is not enough calcium in our bloodstreams, the hormone parathormone takes it from our bones, increasing the risk of a brittle skeleton. Since absorption of calcium decreases with age, the DRI increases as we get older. The calcium DRI between the ages of 19 and 50 is 1,000 milligrams per day, but that number increases to 1,200 milligrams per day when you hit that magic age of 50. Vitamin D helps our bodies absorb calcium from our digestive tract; thus, you should choose a calcium supplement that contains vitamin D.

Since adults may absorb only 30 to 50 percent of ingested calcium, try to spread the intake of calcium-rich foods (as well as supplements) throughout the day to ensure the maximum uptake of this important mineral.

Don't completely shun the sun. Our skin makes vitamin D when our bodies are exposed to ultraviolet B rays from the sun (or tanning booths). There has been such an emphasis on preventing skin cancer and wrinkles that cases of vitamin D insufficiency have been on the rise. The darker your skin, the longer you need to be in the sun to make vitamin D, since the pigment melanin (which gives color to the skin) prevents UV absorption. How much time is enough? Several times a week, expose 25 percent of your body (such as your limbs or arms plus your face) for 25 percent of the time it would take for you to start turning pink in the sun.

Heart disease is the number one killer in the United States, and recent research has emphasized the importance of an amino acid called homocysteine in our blood. The American Heart Association states that too much of it is "related to a higher risk of coronary heart disease, stroke, and peripheral vascular disease (fatty deposits in peripheral arteries)." What does homocysteine actually do? The current thought is that an excess of this amino acid, which is necessary for healthy tissue, can damage blood-vessel linings, leading to the accumulation of plaque, which can block the flow of blood. It has also been implicated in dementia.

Folic acid and vitamins B6 and B12 may break down homocysteine in the bodies of some individuals. Good sources of folic acid include dark green leafy veggies, whole grains, walnuts, and lentils; cereals are often fortified with folic acid. B6 can be found in bananas, nuts, seeds, chicken, and potatoes. Good sources of B12 are eggs, poultry, milk, shellfish, and cottage cheese.

The bottom line is that we need to be informed consumers. New research continues to modify, verify, and vilify prior research. Common sense, knowing what works for you, and maintaining a healthy skepticism will probably serve you well in the nutrition arena.

" . . . AND BE MERRY"

Exercise can make us merrier, but, as with nutrition, you have to find out what works for you. Do you remember the original 1962 Twilight Zone episode "Kick the Can," in which Charles Whitley, residing at the Sunnyvale Rest Home, believed that by thinking young and playing active games (like kick the can), he would truly be young? He was joined by most of Sunnyvale's residents, and indeed, by the end of the show, those who participated in the vigorous game had literally become children once again. (It is the Twilight Zone, remember.) What a powerful statement about the effects of exercise!

Activities you enjoy, performed at a regular time, perhaps with another person who also commits to exercising, offer the best chance to make fitness a lifelong habit. Experts often advise that you exercise first thing in the morning, so that later in the day you don't get too tired or overwhelmed with other things to do and let exercise slide. In other words, insert this valuable activity into your schedule, just as you would grocery shopping, meeting a friend for lunch, or going to a movie; no one can easily find time to exercise. Before embarking on a new exercise regimen or plan, however, it's a good idea to ask your physician to check you out and give you the okay, especially if you have been relatively inactive.

The three pillars of physical fitness are strength training, increasing flexibility, and cardiovascular workouts. Here's a list of some of the benefits of regular exercise.

- Increases feelings of self-worth.
- Reduces LDL ("bad") cholesterol and triglycerides.
- Decreases body fat, including dangerous visceral fat (the fat surrounding organs) that is implicated in diabetes, high blood pressure, and cardiovascular disease.
- Makes your body more sensitive to the effects of insulin, decreasing the chances of developing diabetes.
- Lowers stress levels and relaxes you.
- Helps alleviate moderate levels of depression.
- Elevates mood.
- Improves your appearance.
- Strengthens your heart so it pumps out more

blood with each beat, resulting in a lower heart rate and lightened workload on the heart.

- Lowers blood pressure and decreases the risk of stroke and heart disease.
- Raises your levels of IgA (immunoglobulin A), which fights cold viruses.
- Increases muscular strength and endurance.
- Increases lean body mass, which in turn increases the number of calories your body burns at rest.
- Improves joint flexibility, helping to ease joint pain and stiffness.
- Decreases your chances of getting gallstones.
- Adds or slows loss of bone mass (if it's a weight-bearing exercise), reducing chances of osteoporosis.
- Helps prevent fractures of the spine (back-strengthening exercises in particular).
- Results in the production of a natural antibiotic (dermicidin) by sweat glands.
- Improves blood circulation to the prostate gland.
- Lowers the risk of some cancers, including breast, kidney, endometrial, prostate, and colon cancers.
- Allows you to fall asleep more easily and sleep better.
- Improves the efficiency of the lungs, and delivers more oxygen to cells.
- Decreases risk of falling by improving balance and coordination (yoga is particularly effective).

- Suppresses appetite signals from the hypothalamus after vigorous workouts involving lots of heat production.
- Hones planning, goal-setting, and decision-making skills.
- Increases energy (which may stimulate your sex life as well).

Whew! Although our list is not all-inclusive, you certainly get the idea that exercise is vital to good health!

When we hit our late twenties, we start losing muscle mass—about one percent each year. That doesn't seem like much, but by the time we're 50, we've lost approximately one-fifth of our muscle mass—and replaced a lot of that with fat! Since muscle is much more active metabolically (it burns more calories at rest than fat does), this loss, along with a more sedentary lifestyle, accounts for much of the creeping weight gain as we hit middle age. This weight gain is not inevitable; it can be reversed through lifting weights. In many cases, you can use your own body as the weight (think squats and pushups) or use fairly inexpensive free weights. You don't have to join a club and use their machines (although the social aspect of a club or organized class can be a great extrinsic motivator).

To make sure you're using correct form—not only to prevent injury, but also to get the most out of your workouts—it's a good idea to schedule a few lessons with a personal trainer to put you on the right path.

Call your local health club for some recommendations. Costs vary, but they run somewhere around $50 an hour. Trainers can come to your home or your health club, or you can go to their place of business.

Dr. Miriam Nelson, director of the Center for Physical Fitness at Tufts University in Boston, recommends three 45-minute strength-training workouts a week and three 45-minute aerobic workouts a week. Alternate your strength-training days with aerobic days. Also, stretching while your muscles are warm will promote the best flexibility. If six days of working out seems daunting, start slowly, and see if you can work up to a higher, more intense level. Keep a list of the benefits of working out to help keep you motivated. If you truly believe in the value of exercise, you'll set aside the time. Exercise is something you can't afford not to do!

Remember that a scale is not the only arbiter of change. Although it sounds like a cliché, muscle does weigh more than fat, so as you're becoming more fit, the numbers on the scale may not change that much even though you're losing inches. How you feel, how your clothes fit, and how you look naked standing in front of a full-length mirror are better judges of what's going on with your body! Will you be sore? Most likely. But take this as a good sign that you are producing stronger muscles. As your muscles get more powerful, the soreness will decrease. Of course, actual acute pain is a warning signal from your body that something is wrong. Don't overdo it!

Whether you walk (or mall walk), do yoga, bike, take step aerobics, play tennis or other sports, swim, dance, do core training (strengthening your "core" muscles—your abdominal, back, chest, and shoulder muscles), lift free weights, or use machines, there are a host of rewards from regular exercise. The phrase "use it or lose it" truly applies to keeping your body, an incredible machine, in its best possible shape.

Okay, so you're eating right most of the time and you're exercising several days a week, but you still think the way you look on the outside doesn't reflect how young you feel on the inside. Or you want to have your cake and eat it too (then have it removed from your thighs). Should you consider a cosmetic procedure?

"If I Could Turn Back Time . . ." The title of Cher's song captures the essence of cosmetic surgery—turning back the clock to make our outward appearance more closely resemble the (hopefully!) energetic and vital people we feel we are inside. The American Society of Plastic Surgeons (ASPS) reports that in 2006 about 11 million people had cosmetic procedures, including both surgical procedures (such as a tummy tuck) and nonsurgical cosmetic procedures (such as Botox injections).

ASPS statistics indicate that the top five surgical procedures in 2006 were breast augmentation, rhinoplasty (nose reshaping), liposuction, eyelid surgery, and abdominoplasty (tummy tuck). The most common nonsurgical procedures were Botox injections, chemical peels, laser hair removal, microdermabrasion, and hyaluronic acid (skin fillers).

All this nipping and tucking doesn't come without a cost, however. Most cosmetic surgery is considered elective and will generally not be covered by insurance. In certain cases, such as drooping eyelids that interfere with vision, procedures may be covered. Check with your insurance company to be sure. Payment options may include paying all fees prior to the surgery, making a deposit when scheduling your procedure and paying a penalty for cancellation, using a credit card, or financing your procedure, sometimes through your doctor's office.

Choosing a physician for surgical cosmetic procedures shouldn't be taken lightly. The best advice is to pick a board-certified plastic surgeon. The rigorous credentialing process to become board certified ensures that the surgeon has the necessary training and expertise. Also, consider where the surgery will be performed. Your surgeon should have hospital privileges at the better medical centers. For more extensive surgeries, a medical center is your best bet. Asking friends for suggestions can also be helpful. Your internist or other physicians you see may be a good source for referrals as well. Whatever you do, don't let price be your only factor in choosing a physician for your cosmetic procedures!

The American Society of Plastic Surgeons provides a free referral service for board-certified surgeons by location or name. Go to www.plastic surgery.org and click on "Find a Plastic Surgeon" or call 888-475-2784.

Of course, cosmetic procedures won't change who you are, but they may change how you feel about yourself. If you have realistic expectations about the results, are emotionally stable, recognize the inherent risks, can afford it, and know there will be some discomfort and healing time for some of the procedures, it may be something to consider.

Now, let's look at another way of staying "forever young"—nurturing your emotional health. Feeding your body nutritious food and keeping it in good working condition are very important, but you must nourish the brain and spirit as well.

Your dentist may be able to warn you of an impending stroke! X-rays taken with panoramic machines can detect calcifications in the neck arteries, indicating possible blockages. Alert your dentist to look for this "hardening of the arteries."

THE IMPORTANCE OF GIVING

As we pointed out in Part 1, social support is one ingredient in the recipe for a happier, healthier retirement and a happier, healthier, longer-living you. Research published by Stephanie Brown in *Psychological Science* indicates that it may indeed be healthier to give than to receive. Dr. Brown's study found that "mortality was significantly reduced for individuals who reported providing instrumental support to friends, relatives, and neighbors, and individuals who reported providing emotional support to their spouse." In other words, during this 5-year study of older married adults, those who gave their time and support to others lived longer than those who didn't. Lending a helping hand not only helps others, it increases your longevity.

DOES MARRIAGE MATTER?

Emotional health also benefits from marriage. A recent study from England reported that over a seven-year period, men were more likely to die from being single than from being smokers! Researchers Andrew Oswald and Jonathan Garner from the University of Warwick found that married men had a 6.1 percent lower risk of death than their single counterparts. For married women, the risk of mortality was 2.9 percent lower than for single women. Dr. Oswald summed up, "Forget cash. It is as clear as day from the data that marriage, rather than money, is what keeps people alive." It has been found, however, that unhappy marriages can have a negative effect on health. Depression, ulcers, elevation of stress hormones, increased blood pressure, and even a slower repair of wounds and more cavities have been associated with poor marital relationships. Although the research subjects in these studies were married, it's thought that the same results (good and bad) would also apply to any couple in a long-term, committed relationship.

CONTROLLING STRESS

Our ability to deal with the events life tosses our way can affect our sense of well being. Consider these scenarios: buying a new house, caring for elderly parents, becoming a grandparent, beginning a new career, losing money in the stock market, learning a difficult piece on the piano, preparing for the holidays, being involuntarily downsized, and retiring. How we react to each stimulus determines whether it is a "eustress" (good stress) or a "distress" (bad stress) for us. Eustress, a term coined by Canadian scientist Dr. Hans Selye, can be stimulating, challenging, and fun, while distress can lead to negative consequences such as anxiety, irritability, feelings of being overwhelmed, anger, and depression.

When we experience physical or psychological stress, our bodies churn out the stress hormones cortisol, epinephrine, and norepinephrine, which help regulate insulin; increase blood pressure, heart rate, blood-sugar levels, and blood flow to the large muscles; and prepare us for the "fight-or-flight" response to the stressor. Under ideal circumstances, we experience the stress response, we resolve things, and our levels of stress hormones return to normal. The increase in energy we experience was a beneficial evolutionary response that helped our ancestors escape predators. In modern society, however, the stress response is often initiated repeatedly (think of being stuck in traffic or dealing with an intractable illness), and the body is bathed in these stress chemicals often and for prolonged periods of time, perhaps resulting in fatigue, depression, anxiety, irritability, and pain in the muscles and joints. Older people with chronic stress also tend to have higher levels of a chemical called interleukin-6 that is associated with a decline in immune-system function, as well as illnesses such as heart disease, arthritis, and diabetes.

Frequent negative stress, whether physical or psychological, exacts a toll on the body. One way to reduce stress is to try changing your response to the stressor. One person's distress could be another person's eustress. If you can change the way you perceive a stressor, you can deal with the stress more easily and return your body to its normal state more quickly. Let's say you're committed to doing a half-hour talk for the local Rotary, but you're feeling panicked. Using time management to prepare for your presentation, visualizing yourself making a successful presentation, and practicing your presentation until you feel comfortable could change what would be considered a distress, were you to wing it, to a eustress.

Additional techniques for stress reduction include biofeedback, meditation, slow and deep breathing, exercise (particularly yoga, Pilates, and t'ai chi), massage therapy, getting enough sleep, listening to soothing music or a relaxation tape, interacting with others, making a road map for your life and moving forward on it in measured steps, setting priorities, saying no to unwelcome requests, laughing, surrounding yourself with pink (it's calming) or yellow (energizing), connecting or reconnecting with your spiritual side, associating with positive-thinking people, stretching, practicing aromatherapy (especially with lavender), taking some time for yourself each day, avoiding stressful triggers (for example, keeping a book handy to read while you're on hold on the telephone), taking a walk, learning something new, playing with a pet, making a list of ten things you are grateful for, and practicing mindfulness (a term coined by Dr. Jon Kabat-Zinn, founder and director of the Center for Mindfulness at the University of Massachusetts Medical Center, for giving your full attention to what you're involved in at that particular time).

Finally, remember that you are responsible for your own feelings; you are in charge of choosing your response to emotional stimuli. Replace flawed thinking (life "must" be fair; you "must" treat me like a king/queen; I "must" be perfect in all I do) with rational thought processes (I "prefer" that life is fair, but even though it isn't, I can still enjoy it; I "prefer" that you treat me like a queen, but I can't control your actions; I "prefer" that I never make a mistake, but when I do, I know I'm still an okay person). Practicing this kind of thinking is called cognitive behavioral therapy or rational emotive behavior therapy. Try it; it works! But it takes time and practice to replace negative, ingrained thought patterns with newer, healthier ones. The payoff? A lot less stress in your life.

Let's face it—a life that is completely stress-free would be boring, but too much stress is unhealthy.

AVOIDING DEPRESSION

Depression among older adults is frequently overlooked. In fact, it's estimated that three out of 100 people over 65 experience clinical depression. Sometimes there may be no obvious cause for the depression, or it may be the result of a change (decline in health, loss of spouse, retirement, etc.); certain medications may also mimic or cause depression. If you think you or someone you know is depressed, it's important to seek help from your physician or a mental-health professional and to stick with treatment options until a successful one is found.

KEEPING YOUR BRAIN FIT

When we discuss staying forever young, we can't ignore the care of the three-pound dynamo called the brain. Comprising about two percent of our weight but consuming close to 20 percent of our energy needs, this vital organ needs to be kept in the best shape possible. It had been, for about a century, a basic tenet in biology that brain cells don't regenerate—that once the brain matures, we have all the neurons we're ever going to have, and we can only lose them. Research done in the past decade, however, has upended this belief, and we now know that new cell growth has been observed in the most advanced parts of the brain involving learning and memory. So, how do you keep your brain in fighting form?

Researchers from the University of Illinois at Champaign-Urbana presented some interesting findings at the 2006 annual meeting of the American Psychological Association. They reported that aerobic activity had both short and long-term effects, including improved mental functioning and a reduced risk of dementia and Alzheimer's. It's thought that physical activity actually affects the brain at the cellular level by providing more blood flow to those areas involved in memory and stimulating the growth of neurons. So aerobic exercise can keep both brain and body buff!

In addition to physical exercise, mental gymnastics may play a role in keeping our brains facile. One type of mental exercise is called "neurobics." A cute play on words, coined by Dr. Lawrence Katz and Manning Rubin by combining the word for brain cells, neuron, with the word aerobic, as in aerobic exercise, neurobics involves using your senses in ways you usually don't, doing something novel, and/or changing a routine. Switching hands to brush your teeth or to write, learning to play an instrument, studying a foreign language, taking a different route to a frequent destination, or getting dressed with your eyes closed are examples of neurobic exercises; these activities stimulate your neurons and rev up neglected nerve pathways.

More suggestions for maintaining your mental edge: Get sufficient sleep; don't smoke; be aware of side effects of medications; do crossword puzzles, brainteasers, acrostics, and riddles; avoid extreme stress; play bridge or chess; be socially engaged with others; read; listen to music; play board games; garden; dance; and travel. Then, of course, there is the Japanese puzzle craze of Sudoku, or Nintendo's *Brain Age*.

> Be sure you incorporate variety and novelty into your brain workouts. You need to cross train your brain like you cross train your body; pursuing a single activity, such as Sudoku, for 5 hours a day doesn't provide the brain with enough different kinds of stimulation. "Use it or lose it" applies as much to the brain as to the body.

SOURCES

AIG SunAmerica. Re-Visioning Retirement Survey. 2002.

Carter, Mary Anne, and Kelli Cook. 1995. "Adaptation to retirement: role changes and psychological resources." *The Career Development Quarterly* 44:67–82.

Firebaugh, Glen. 2005. "Relative increased happiness: Are Americans on a hedonic treadmill?" Paper presented at the American Sociological Centennial Annual Meeting.

Giles, Lynn et al, 2005. "Effect of social networks on 10-year survival in very old Australians." *Journal of Epidemiology and Community Health* 59:574–9.

Giltay, Erik et al, 2006. "Higher optimism levels associated with lower risk of cardiovascular death in elderly men." *Archives of Internal Medicine* 166:431-436.

Glass, Thomas, et al. 1999. "Population-based study of social and productive activities as predictors of survival among elderly Americans." *British Medical Journal* 319(8):478–83.

Holtzman, Elizabeth. University of Massachusetts. "Retirement: The Emotional Aspects." 4 April 2002. www.umass.edu/fsap/articles/retire.html.

Joens-Matre, R. R., and Ekkekakis, P. 2002. "Can short walks enhance affect in older adults?" *Journal of Sport & Exercise Psychology* 24: S75–76.

Lorraine Dorfman. 2002. "Stayers and leavers: professors in an era of no mandatory retirement." *Educational Gerontology* 28(1):15–33.

Lykken, David, and Auke Tellegen. 1996. "Happiness is a stochastic phenomenon." *Psychological Science* 7(3):188–89.

Michael, Yvonne, et al. 2001. "Living arrangements, social integration, and change in functional health status." *American Journal of Epidemiology* 153(1):123–31.

Moen, Phyllis, et al. 2001. "Couples' work/retirement transitions, gender, and marital quality." *Social Psychology Quarterly* 64(1):55–71.

Moen, Phyllis, William A. Erickson, Madhurima Agarwal, Vivian Fields, and Laurie Todd. *The Cornell Retirement and Well-Being Study: Final Report.* Ithaca, New York: Bronfenbrenner Life Course Center, Cornell University, 2000.

Ostir, Kenneth et al. 2004. "Onset of frailty in older adults and the protective role of positive affect." *Psychology and Aging.* 19(1).

Wilson, Sven E. 2002. "The health capital of families: an investigation of the inter-spousal correlation in health status." *Social Science and Medicine* 55:1157–1172.

If you have enjoyed this book,
Hallmark would love to
hear from you.

Hallmark Book Feedback

P.O. Box 419034

Mail Drop 215

Kansas City, MO 64141

booknotes@hallmark.com